*A Life*
# On the Black River
*In Arkansas*

# *A Life*
# On the Black River
## *In Arkansas*

**The memoir of a farmer,
rural entrepreneur, and banker**

## E. R. Coleman
*as told to Mary Frances Hodges*

The Butler Center for Arkansas Studies

**BUTLER**
**CENTER**

**BOOKS**

The Butler Center for Arkansas Studies
Central Arkansas Library System
100 Rock Street
Little Rock, Arkansas 72201

Book design and cover art: H. K. Stewart

Front and back cover photographs: Wallace Lytle, 1957

ISBN (hardcover): 978-1-935106-04-3
ISBN (paperback): 978-1-935106-06-7
Library of Congress PCN: 2008927763

10 9 8 7 6 5 4 3 2 1

Printed in the United States of America.

To my wife, Florene

# Acknowledgments

When I was a young man, I was raised by parents who knew what it was to struggle for the necessities of life, and who had the will to survive under difficult circumstances. My parents had very little formal education. However, they had a good education through honest work and wisdom. To them, work had no boundaries because of one's background, and I learned to be mature at an early age. I had dreams and goals for my life early on. As a young man, I was privileged to have many leaders and mentors who took an interest in me and encouraged me.

I wanted to be a good man, have a good marriage, good children, and lots of good friends, and I wanted to be successful in life. I have been blessed beyond measure by my family, my wife, Florene, and my three children, Carol, Kathryn, and Donald. My three children have earned college degrees. Whether or not I am a good man is for God to decide.

No person has had more or better friends than I have had, and I want to thank every person who has touched my life. It has been my belief that there is good in every person. I try to take the good from every person to my advantage and leave the rest to someone else. I have wanted to be a "little bit" of every person I meet.

In writing this book, my intent has been to tell about my life experiences as they related to the social, economic, and cultural changes in Arkansas, eastern Independence County, and the Black River Swamp area. I hope I have accomplished that.

This book may not have been written at all had it not been for my daughter Carol Beth Coleman-Kennedy. Following my open heart surgery some 10 years ago, she said to me,

"Daddy, you are going to be sitting in that chair and looking at these four walls for the next six weeks. Why don't you write a book? You have seen lots of things and done lots of things. When you are gone, we won't know how things were unless you write them."

So I want to thank her for encouraging me to write this book about personal experiences of my life. I am including stories that demonstrate changes in eastern Independence County, Arkansas, over the past 100 years or so. I also want to thank those who contributed pictures, memories, and helpful stories.

I want to thank Mrs. Mary Frances Hodges, my writer and editor, for her patience in writing and re-writing the material I gave her. I also want to thank the late Mr. Clyde McGinnis for his contribution and help with his material and memories. Thanks, also, to Mr. Dale Cole of First Community Bank of Batesville, Arkansas, for allowing me to launch the distribution of this book in the bank's lobby.

To my dear, beloved wife, Lois Florene Hugg Coleman, for her patience, love, and support through all our years together, I give special thanks.

Most appreciated, also, are the late Wilson Powell of the *Batesville Guard* newspaper, for writing helpful articles on behalf of this book, and to Charles Osborne, Commander, U.S. Navy (Retired), for his kind remarks in writing the Foreword.

This book would not have been possible without the help of all of these people. I am grateful to each of them.

There can be no definition of a successful life unless it includes service to others.

# Table of Contents

# Foreword

This book gives a fascinating look at life in days past in northeast Arkansas beginning in the 1920s and 1930s until the present time. E. R. Coleman is a close friend whom I have known almost all of my life. I know E. R. to be honest and trustworthy. He is not afraid to accept responsibility, and his word is his bond.

He helped his father clear the timber from land which he later farmed with horses and mules. They raised their own milk cows, beef cattle, hogs, poultry, fruits, and vegetables.

These efforts were instrumental in forming the character traits within E. R. that contributed to his achievements. Growing up in hard times conditioned him to visualize better and more progressive ways of doing things, which he implemented in his own farming operation.

He started his education in a one-room school, later graduating as salutatorian from Strawberry High School in Lawrence County, Arkansas. After high school, he married Lois Florene Hugg, and they have two daughters, Carol Beth and Kathryn, and a son, Donald.

E. R. and Florene were very active members of the Cord Baptist Church where he served as a deacon for more than 20 years. He also served on the Board of Directors for Independence County's Soil and Water Conservation District for over 20 years. In 1967, he was selected as the State Director of that organization.

As E. R.'s farming operation grew, he bought several thousand additional acres of land which he developed and operated as E. R. Coleman Farms, Inc. He also operated Coleman Seed Company. He produced and bought hybrid seed, which he sold throughout the South and in foreign countries.

In addition, he bought controlling interest in First National Bank of Batesville. He also owned controlling interest in First Bank Holding Company of Batesville, along with four branch banks.

At age 82, he has yet to retire, always moving ahead with new, innovative ideas and projects.

You might ask: "Can anything good come out of Cord-Dowdy, Arkansas?" The answer is "Yes, and his name is Ewell Ray Coleman."

Commander Charles Osborne
U.S. Navy (Retired)

# You Have to Have a Toehold

My father, Ewell Winfred Coleman, always said, "Everybody somewhere down in life has got to have a toehold. You have to have a toehold before you can do anything. If you're going to climb a mountain, and even if you're the best mountain climber in the world, you have to have that first toehold. You stick your toe in that first toehold and then get another toehold a little higher up, another one a little higher than that. If you don't get that first toehold, you are never going to climb a mountain."

My first toehold was my parents and the town of Cord, Arkansas. Cord is not the most famous town in the state, or even Independence County, but the most important to me. My parents and the Cord community helped raise me. I have deep roots in this area. My great grandparents, George and Rebecca Coleman, moved from North Carolina via Weakley County, Tennessee, and homesteaded in Independence County in 1853. They bought land from W. H. Cowell in Township 14, Range 3 West, Section 17.

In 1853, George Coleman owned four slaves. However, the 1860 Slave Census for Independence County shows that George owned only two slaves, ages 15 and 17. Family tradition says that all four slaves were a family unit with the parents of the younger slaves having died.

George and Rebecca Coleman had a son, Wesley Robert Coleman. He was born in Tennessee in 1833. When he was about 17 or 18 years old, he moved with his family to Independence County, Arkansas. He married Haseltine T. Gold in 1860, and they lived in the Oak Ridge vicinity of Cord. He was a farmer and owned considerable amounts of land.

Wesley Robert enlisted in the Confederate Army in the spring of 1863. He was a Private in Company K of Colonel R. J. Shaver's Regiment, Arkansas Infantry, CSA. He was captured at DeVall's Bluff 17 August 1863 and was sent to prison at Alton, Illinois. In 1864, he appears on the prisoners' roll at Fort Delaware. He was then sent to City Point, Virginia, where he was exchanged for Union prisoners on 7 March 1865. He was paroled at Jacksonport, Arkansas, 6 June 1865.

Following the war, he owned and operated a mule-powered cotton gin located south of what was later the homeplace of Don Coleman, a great grandson. My father, Ewell Winfred Coleman, said they were able to gin three bales of cotton per day. Ginning was paid by taking a toll of one-tenth of the cotton to be ginned.

Wesley Coleman's wife, Haseltine, was the first member of the Cumberland Presbyterian Church at Cord and the registrar of all deaths. Wesley Coleman was an elder in the Cord Presbyterian Church and assistant superintendent of the Sabbath School. All of their children were born in Cord. One of their sons, William David Coleman, was my grandfather.

William David Coleman married my grandmother, Laurinda R. Winston, on 23 November 1892. Laurinda was born in Cord, and her parents were Thomas Columbus and Mary Francis Winston. Before the Winstons left North Carolina to move west, they donated property for the public buildings in what is now Winston-Salem, North Carolina.

William David and Laurinda Coleman were members of the Oak Ridge Methodist Church at Cord. After Laurinda's death in 1935, William married Minnie Douglas Clinton, widow of James E. Clinton.

Ewell Winfred, my dad, was the son of William and Laurinda Coleman and was born 21 August 1901. Essentially, all the Coleman families since 1853 were born in

Independence County, and most are buried in Hopewell Cemetery at Cord.

People have asked, "How did Cord get its name?" It was supposed to be called "McCord" after a Mr. J. V. McCord who organized the Hopewell Church in 1836. When the local officials attempted to file the papers for a post office, there was already a post office in Arkansas named "McCord." So, the name was shortened to "Cord." It is in Black River Township, which was created while Arkansas was still part of the Missouri Territory.

My father was six years older than my mother. They were married in 1923. My father courted her in his horse and buggy, which was equivalent to a Cadillac in those days. With that rig, he could have gotten any girl he wanted, but he chose my mother, Hazel Estella Greer. Mother had a teaching certificate. Prior to their marriage, Mother taught school at the one-room school in Walnut Grove.

My mother was born in 1907. She and her family lived in Jackson County at the time my parents married. My mother's father, Campbell Greer, died in the 1918 flu epidemic. He took sick after transporting a good friend's coffin to the cemetery in the pouring rain. My mother was 11 years old. She was the fifth of seven children. The seventh child was born shortly after her father's death.

My parents built a little house on a hillside east of what was called "Granddad Coleman's place" on some land they purchased from him. I was born in that little house on 12 October 1925—Columbus Day. I am surprised they didn't name me Columbus. I often considered myself a "Columbus boy," because I have ventured into uncharted areas.

After my parents built their house, Dad decided he wanted a well close to the back door so he could conveniently step out back and get a drink of water. Before he started digging the well, he solicited the help of a water witch. Back then, people wouldn't dig wells without going to a person in the community who was supposed to have magical power to locate well water.

The water witch took a forked, peach tree limb, holding the forked ends and pointing the straight part in front of him. Supposedly, when the water witch stepped across a stream of underground water, the straight limb would turn down toward the ground. I have heard it said that it would twist off the bark in your hand moving up and down over a stream of water. You could gauge how far down the water was by how many times the limb moved up and down. So Daddy hired a water witch to come and find the water.

The water witch walked all over that hillside, the back yard, and around the house. He couldn't find any water. The water witch told Daddy, "Mr. Coleman, there ain't no water here around the house." So he wandered off down the hill. Down under the hill where it leveled off, that peach tree limb threw a fit moving up and down. The water witch advised Daddy to dig his well there, and he would get water. However, there was a big problem: it was a long distance from the house to the well, and water would have to be carried up the hill the rest of his life.

Daddy paid the water witch and went back to the house. He announced he was going to dig a well at the back door. And that he did.

Daddy did his own digging, and Mother hoisted the dirt and gravel in a bucket to the top of the ground with the help of a hand windlass my dad made. Toward the bottom of the well, Daddy hit hard gravel that was just like concrete. Dad would hit that packed gravel with a pick and knock loose one little piece. It would bounce up and hit him on the shin. He worked with that pick intensely for about a week without much progress. He had to stand in an awkward position because the walls of the well sloped into a V-shape and there was hardly room to stand at the bottom. Nevertheless, he was determined to have a well at his back door.

Dad attempted several times to dynamite the hard-packed gravel, but that didn't help much, either. Dad didn't know anything about handling dynamite. He wasn't an expert in anything but hard work and good advice. There was a man in another community who was an expert in handling dynamite, so Dad hired him.

The man started to work the next Monday. He and Dad worked all morning to no avail. Mother called them to dinner, which was the noon meal in those days. The man said, "Mr. Coleman, before we go eat, let's finish this." The man set the charge of dynamite so the smoke would be cleared when they finished dinner. That way, they could dig farther. During the dinner meal, the dynamite went off with a little thud sound. Dad was really disappointed, because he'd expected a loud noise that could be heard on the back side of the farm two acres away. He felt sure he wasted his hard-earned money.

After dinner, they went back to the well. It was obvious the man knew what he was talking about. He had strategically placed the charges where they needed to be, and the wall of the well was straight up and down. That afternoon, they made more progress digging than Dad had made in two weeks. Daddy was happy about spending his hard-earned money.

So, Daddy had his well exactly where he wanted it. It continues to be one of the finest wells in the country today, and the well was dug in 1925. This story validates the old adage "You get what you pay for."

My dad didn't have much money, but he was a hard-working man, and he was honest and trustworthy. His word was his bond. Dad always told me, "Ewell, you might not have nothing, but if you will be honest and willing to work, you're going to make it. There will be somebody who will recognize that kind of a trait in a man and give you a job. You have to be trustworthy." That was Dad's philosophy, and I think that's good advice for anybody. That advice is worth more than money. Dad instilled in me the desire to be honest and the desire to work, and he taught me to give a man a day's work for a day's pay—and then some. "Be willing to go the second mile before you go the first mile," he said. It paid off for me!

Back in those days, Cord was well blessed with three doctors: Dr. McAdams, Dr. Rice, and Dr. Brown. Dr. Rice lived on the edge of the southwest trail at Hazel Grove, and his office was in his house. Dr. Brown delivered me, and he lived at Charlotte. Dr. McAdams lived in Cord. In the early 1940s, the Cord 4-H Club established a park and honored Dr. McAdams by naming it McAdams Park.

When I was a toddler, my dad and mother worked together in the fields. Mother plowed as much as my dad did. I stayed with my grandmother, Laurinda Coleman. I was learning to walk while stabilizing myself by holding onto furniture. One day at dinnertime, I was holding onto the table, and I pulled myself to the place where Grandmother had placed a big bowl of hot sauerkraut. I was tall enough to get my little fingers over the edge of the bowl of sauerkraut. I jerked the bowl and turned it upside down on top of my head. I was badly burned. My head was scalded, and the hot sauerkraut lodged around my shirt collar and into my shirt.

Dad took me to Dr. McAdams, who treated my burned head, neck, and shoulder with mercurochrome. Of course, the wounds got dry, hard, and scaly. My dad told me he held me day and night for two weeks because I cried and screamed in severe pain.

Eventually, my crying began to wear on Dad's patience, and he was frustrated with the whole situation. He begged Dr. McAdams to change my medication and said, "We're going to have to do something else besides mercurochrome." Dr. McAdams hum-hawed around and said, "Well, now, Win, I'm trying to doctor that kid to where he won't have very many scars, and if we do something else, he will be scarred up real bad." Daddy said, "Well, if we don't do something else, he's going to die, so why do the scars make any difference?" So Dr. McAdams changed the medication. I have the scars to prove it, and I'm still living. To this day, I have a deep scar on my left shoulder the size of the palm of my hand. I'll carry that scar to my grave. As a consequence of that accident, I didn't have any hair on my head until I was five years old.

* * *

Looking back over my lifetime these 82 years, I realize my father not only was a determined man, he also was a progressive thinker and doer. In his day, Dad would have been considered a real pioneer. He had a fourth-grade education, I think, and was always in favor of something good. Dad was wise. He knew what was good and stayed away from the bad. He actively supported better education, especially with his children, and was a strong promoter of good schools. He wanted better opportunities for people than he had.

Dad wanted a good church in his community. There was an old, wooden church at Cord that was built high off the ground. Hogs slept under the floor of the church. During one of the night services, Dad told the story about the Ku Klux Klan coming through the church shrouded in their white sheets. They walked in the front door and down the aisle, momentarily stood in front of the preacher, and walked out the back door without saying a word. Nothing happened. I suppose they wanted the community to know they were in the neighborhood.

In 1934, my family moved north of Cord to the community of Dowdy. I was nine years old. Some people around Dowdy community were not very civilized, or at least they didn't act that way. No one stood up to their unruly behavior. My dad wouldn't tolerate a lot of things happening around Dowdy. He wanted to have a church and a school. He wanted a community that was progressive, and some folks around there had not been challenged to strive for better things. They certainly didn't want outsiders coming in telling them what to do and not do. They didn't want to change the way they had been doing things all those years. It was evident from their behavior they didn't want a school, and they didn't want a church. They ran away a preacher, and a student whipped a teacher so badly that she had to be hospitalized.

One night during church service, a big rock suddenly came hurtling through the church window shattering glass everywhere. The rock was soon followed by a five-gallon bucket of water doused on my sister, Winona. She was drenched. That would never do! The next day, my dad and the sheriff arrested the man who was responsible for the damages and made him pay a fine.

That wasn't the only time my dad and the sheriff made outlaws pay a fine. One night during church services, a group of boys and men rode their horses round and round the church shooting their guns in the air. The next day, Dad and the sheriff rounded up the guys, once again, making them pay a fine.

Justice of the Peace Court sessions were treated as if they were a community holiday. Everyone in the community came and brought their kids. One of the most memorable court sessions started with an incident at church the night before. A man in the community wandered into a church meeting drunk as a hoot owl. During the service, he threw his bottle of whiskey across the room, hitting the opposite wall, and quite naturally, the church service was over. The next day, the constable made sure the man appeared at the Justice of the Peace Court. Henry Crigler was the justice of the peace, and court was held at his house. A man in the crowd demanded to know the evidence against his friend. Mr. Crigler held up a pint whiskey bottle that was about one-third full. The man asked to see the evidence, and the bottle was passed to him. He immediately turned up the bottle and drank the remainder of the whiskey, thus destroying the evidence. Needless to say, court was adjourned.

One of the troublemakers repeatedly did things my dad wouldn't tolerate. He often seemed to be paying fines or appearing before the Justice of the Peace Court. His actions were unpredictable. There was no telling what he might do next. For instance, people used to have "dinner on the ground" after church. I wasn't there to see this, but I'm told at one of those church dinners, beautifully home-cooked food was served on wooden plank tables in the church yard. Out of nowhere came a man riding his horse as fast as he could, and he jumped his horse over the tables. People scattered in all directions, but luckily, no one was injured and food remained intact on the tables.

Despite this guy's unpredictable behavior and deeds of misconduct, he consistently went to my dad's grocery store to buy food. If he needed money or groceries on credit, my dad would either loan or give it to him. When he died, my dad was probably his best friend.

* * *

Getting a church organized at Dowdy was no easy task. There were two churches at Strawberry 10 miles north of Dowdy, the Church of Christ and a Baptist church. Both congregations wanted to start a church in the Dowdy area. They used the Stone School House for church services which was three-fourths of a mile north of Dowdy. One of the preachers would visit the community and try to promote interest, and then the preacher from the other church would come and do the same. After much visiting, frustration, and rejection, one of the missionary preachers commented that the front door of the Stone School House was 10 feet away from the gates of hell. Later, the Baptist church established a congregation at the Stone School House.

I think one reason for strife and disharmony in this territory was that everyone was either a river rat or a hillbilly, and the two were incompatible. River rats didn't allow hillbillies in the bottom land, and hillbillies didn't allow river rats in the hill land. Eastern Independence County was part swamp land and part hill land.

Sometimes, the young people would round up a fiddler and have a dance, although some of the church people frowned on it. The young people from the bottoms would have their dance, and the young people from the hills would have a separate dance. If a boy from the bottoms started making eyes at a hill girl, or if a boy from the hills became friendly with a girl from the bottoms, there was going to be a fight. Every community had its bully, and a bully from the hills and a bully from the bottoms would fight to settle the matter while half killing each other.

* * *

The first post office in this area was at Lockhart Point, locally called "Pansy" and later named McGill. McGill was a thriving community with a sawmill camp and a steamboat landing. The mail had to be delivered by steamboat, as the only road to Lockhart was a wagon road through the swamps. Albert Wilson was the postmaster at McGill in 1925. Later, the McGill post office moved to a grocery store located on an old wagon road in the foothills near the Stone School House.

This location is about a quarter of a mile behind what is now my house. Many rural grocery stores were not money-making propositions in and of themselves. The store needed a post office in order to survive.

That particular grocery store burned. The post office was moved to a store owned by Bev Matheny and was renamed Black River Post Office. Bev's wife, Rosie Matheny, was named postmistress. Bev Matheny's store and Black River Post Office was located in a field one mile north of where my house is now.

In 1930, Mr. Matheny decided to sell his store to Grover White from Lynn, Arkansas. Mr. White built a new building about a mile up the road. My mother was appointed postmistress. This time, the post office was named Dowdy.

Dad later bought the store from Mr. White. Once or twice a month, Dad took a truckload of groceries and supplies down to the Lockhart landing to get the shell diggers' business. The shell diggers gathered at Lockhart landing to meet the "fast boats" (boats with a gas motor) going upstream to the button factory at Black Rock. There'd be a big gathering, and after the shell diggers sold all their collected mussel shells, they had a little money to spend. So Dad was there to sell them whatever they needed. Shelling was big business at one time on the Black River.

We also operated a grist mill in connection with our store. People could have their own wheat and corn ground. I have ground many a bushel of wheat and corn at our mill. The people didn't have any money, so we took a "toll" for every sack of grain we ground. A "toll" amounted to a big scoop of the ground grain, which was a pre-arranged agreement between the buyer and seller. Then we took the toll amount to the store and put it in the bin for people who wanted to buy a small amount.

Dad added a blacksmith shop with the help of Claude Simpson who became the first blacksmith there. Mr. Simpson lived in the Lick Skillet community in Independence County. The next blacksmith was Luther Gray.

We also had a pooling pen close to the store. People who had five pigs or so to sell could keep them in the pen until other people brought their pigs. When enough pigs were pooled to pay for shipping, the pigs were transported to St. Louis, Missouri, to sell.

The ledger book from our store shows the prices of various items in 1939: coal oil 25 cents, bread 10 cents, sugar 25 cents, and coffee 25 cents.

My mother was the postmistress at Dowdy for 38 years. It was the last fourth-class post office to be closed in Independence County, thanks to Congressman Wilbur Mills. Mother could have retired after 20 years, but she chose not to. My dad and I went to see Mr. Mills at his Searcy Office, and he said the next time a memo came across his desk about closing Dowdy post office, he'd just put it in the trash basket. Mother finally retired when she found out she could make more money from government retirement than she was making while working.

Jim Barnett, a long-time family friend, said that he never saw my mother sitting down. She was always in motion taking care of customers, putting the mail into the boxes, and taking care of her family. The customer window, post office boxes, and many supplies from Dowdy Post Office are on display at the Old Independence Regional Museum in Batesville.

The country store did more than sell groceries and handle the mail. It also served as the community center. On Saturday nights, my dad laid wooden planks over wood blocks and arranged them theatre style in the center of the store. The neighbors would gather to listen to *Lum and Abner* on the radio on Saturday night. There would be eight to 10, iron-wheeled wagons and teams tied to the trees outside. Listening to that radio show was the primary form of entertainment in those days. We were the first family in Dowdy to have electricity, and the first radio—and much later, the first television.

* * *

The first school I attended was at Oak Ridge. My first and finest teacher ever was Miss Elsie Moore at Oak Ridge. Later, I attended school at the Stone School House, which was a one-room school house, as most rural schools were in that day. All eight grades were taught there. The teacher was Earnest Sexton. I have often said that if you sit in a one-room school for eight years and hear the teacher teach all eight grades, and you can't pass eighth-grade math at the end of that time, you haven't been paying attention.

The only spanking I ever received in school was when attending school at the Stone School House. My best friend was Marvin West, and my brother Van Doyne's best friend was Paul Sexton. One day we built an Indian tepee and covered it with dry sage grass, which we pulled out of an adjoining field. When we finished, Van Doyne and Paul wouldn't let us in. I asked Marvin if he had a match. He didn't have one, but said he would go get one, and he did. So I set fire to the tepee. Everyone knows what dry sage grass will do when it is lit with fire. It burns like gasoline. I guess you could say we smoked them out fast. The fire burned all of the field near the school house before it could be contained. Mr. Sexton took the belt to me right up on stage in front of the students. I deserved it!

I wasn't the only mischief maker, though. Each student took turns putting his or her waste paper in the pot-bellied stove. When it came my friend's turn, he not only put his waste paper into the stove, but also a handful of .22 rifle shells. It wasn't long before the shells started exploding, and it sounded as if popping corn were in the stove. Nothing bad happened as a result of the prank. It was just a little mischievous fun.

The Stone School House holds a special place in the hearts of the people who attended school there. Mr. Jim Stone and his wife donated two acres of land for the school house. They each signed the deed with their "X" mark, as neither could read or write. The community honored Mr. and Mrs. Stone by naming the school after them. The Stone School House was restored in 2001. More than 100 people came to the dedication ceremony, some from as far away as Chicago, Illinois.

I went to high school at Strawberry. The high school at Strawberry had started out as an academy, and families from 30 to 40 miles around would pay tuition to have their children attend there. The children who lived long distances away boarded with families in the area.

I guess I could be called an overachiever, but I have always had the opinion that whatever you're going to do, do your best and give it all you've got. As a student at Strawberry High School, I was president of the student body, the salutatorian of my senior class, and president of Future Farmers of America (FFA). Later on as a young man, I was honored as Star Farmer of America, Arkansas State Farmer, and Southeastern United States Regional Farmer of the Year. My leadership training was largely influenced by my mentors, peers, and teachers at Strawberry High School.

Strawberry was one of the few schools in the state that had classes in Vocational Agriculture. Mr. Albert McBride was the agriculture teacher, and Mr. Earl Landers was the area supervisor. Mr. Landers was one of the finest men I ever met, and he was my mentor.

In August 1947, my sister, Winona, received a letter stating that she was the first girl in the State of Arkansas to receive a scholarship in the field of Vocational Home Making at the University of Arkansas. After graduation, she married Wilson Penn from Lynn, Arkansas. They moved to Missouri, and she worked as a home economics teacher and Wilson as a guidance counselor. Wilson was head of the Missouri State Teachers' Association for many years.

Strawberry was noted as a learning center primarily because of the progressive leadership and influence of many people, including Lawrence Sloan and his wife, Harriet "Hatz" Padgett Sloan, of the Padgett Lumber Company in Batesville.

* * *

Another individual who promoted education and influenced Strawberry School was my dad. He bought a school bus to transport the kids in the Dowdy area to the Strawberry School where all 12 grades were available. Actually, he bought a bus chassis in Batesville that consisted of the underframe, an engine, a steering column, and steering wheel. There was no protection from the weather, not even a windshield. So Dad and a neighbor friend, Monroe Douglas, sat on boxes, and they drove the chassis to Fort Wayne, Indiana, to have the rest of the bus assembled. Then they drove home in comfort, so to speak.

Owning a school bus was not intended to be a money-making deal. There wasn't any money to be had anyway. Daddy bought the school bus to be sure that his sons and daughter would be in a good school at 0800 on a school day, and if anybody else in the neighborhood wanted to ride, they were welcome. That was my dad's attitude. He wanted other children in the surrounding area to have a good education, too. So he drove up and down Highway 25 collecting kids and transporting them up to the Strawberry School. Some of the neighbors would pay him a small fee to carry their kids to school.

Highway 25 was a gravel road in those days, which was a big improvement compared to what it had been. Dad helped gravel Highway 25, which replaced part of the old military road that ran from St. Louis, Missouri, to Arkansas Post in south Arkansas. When Highway 25 was built, road-building machinery and equipment was not available as it is today, so men built it with dirt scoops pulled by mules. They shoveled the gravel into a wagon with poles in the bottom of the wagon bed. After the wagon was filled with gravel, they pulled it from one spot to the next. The men raised those poles up out of the wagon bed and let the gravel dump onto the road. Men built Highway 25 with manual labor, a shovel, and a wagon. Today Highway 25 is blacktop.

One day in the early part of Daddy's school bus venture, the Strawberry Superintendent of Schools stepped on the bus as Dad drove up. He said, "Mr. Coleman, this afternoon when you pick up the kids, I want you to put the boys on one side and the girls on the other. Daddy said, "Sir, I don't know if I can do that. And besides, I wasn't hired to separate the boys and the girls. (Actually, Dad wasn't hired by anyone.) If you want that done, you're welcome to do it yourself."

Later that morning, Daddy went to Austin Nichols, who was president of the school board, and said, "Austin, when I unloaded the kids at school this morning, the superintendent stepped into the bus and told me to separate the boys and the girls by putting the boys on one side of the bus and the girls on the other. Now, if the school board tells me to do that, well then, I'm going to tell you just like I told the superintendent. You're welcome to do that yourself, and I'm quitting right now."

Mr. Nichols said, "Ah, Win, that will blow over. You go on. We'll take care of that." So that afternoon, Daddy came back to the school house to pick up the kids. You know how kids are when school is over. They will "break their neck," so to speak, to get out of the school house door to get in the bus. And so the kids loaded onto the bus, and the superintendent came prancing out. He stepped inside the door of the bus and looked around. He said, "Mr. Coleman, I thought I told you this morning to separate these boys and girls. Put the girls on one side, and the boys on the other."

Daddy said, "Yeah, Sir, you told me that, but don't you remember? I told you I couldn't do that, and if you want it done, you're welcome to do it yourself. I'll wait here while you do it."

So the superintendent proceeded to separate the boys and the girls. He yanked up three or four boys from their seats and moved them to the other side of the bus and moved three or four girls to the opposite side. When he got to the third row from the front, he encountered a great big, overgrown, redneck boy and proceeded to move him to the other side. That boy stood straight up, clenched his fist, and socked the superintendent on the jaw. Needless to say, that put a stop to separating the boys from the girls.

* * *

We human beings are pretty much set in our ways. It takes a lot of persuasion to change our attitudes about things. The way we perceive things may be right, or it may be wrong. It takes a lot of education, time, and pain for people to change. We learn at our own pace. There's an old saying, "A man who's changed against his will is of the same opinion still."

In the late 1930s ('37 or '38), the Rural Electric Association (REA) came into being. Mr. Lawrence Sloan of Strawberry was appointed to the first national board of directors of the REA. Of course, Mr. Sloan wanted one of the first REA districts to be in his area of Arkansas. He proceeded to develop what we know now as Craighead Electric, the same cooperative that's furnishing electricity to us today. Back then, the REA had to get three committed customers' signatures per mile to qualify for building the electric line.

Mr. Sloan asked Dad if he would be willing to use his school bus to help transport people to various towns so they could hear about the possibility of getting electricity. Mr. Sloan would come over to our house and say, "Mr. Coleman, this Saturday I'd like for you to go to Marianna and pick up a load of people and transport them to Jonesboro, or to Paragould or to Little Rock or wherever, so we can try to persuade them to become REA customers over this five-county district in northeast Arkansas." My dad transported people to meetings all over northeast Arkansas, trying to educate, persuade, and sell the people on the idea that electricity would be a good thing.

Most people had kerosene lamps. A few people owned Delco generators. Generators had to be started about 3:00 in the afternoon to build up enough energy to have lights in the evening. Around 10:00 p.m., the lights started getting dim, gradually diminishing to no lights at all. The next day around 3:00 in the afternoon, generators had to be started again so people could have lights again at night. Basically, everybody used kerosene lamps, which also meant hot water was not available, except what was heated on the wood-burning stove. There was no indoor plumbing, just outhouses for toilets and chamber mugs beside the bed, in case you needed to go "to the bathroom" in the middle of the night. Until the last year or two of high school, we had school by kerosene lamps, and then we progressed to an Aladdin Lamp which was twice as bright. Our first refrigerator was fueled with kerosene, and our Maytag washing machine had a gas engine.

Mr. Sloan worked for about two years trying to form the rural Northeast Arkansas electrification district. My dad worked religiously on the project. He did everything he could to help get the program started. We lived about five miles from the county line between Independence and Lawrence County. There was not one person in the last four miles that would take electricity, except for my dad. Twelve to 15 patrons were needed to qualify for the electric line to be run down to my dad's store. Dad was getting really depressed because no one would help him get electricity into the area. People would say things like, "Man, that electricity is poisonous." "Liable to blow up." "I hear it gives you cancer." "The cows won't give milk." They were invariably resistant to change.

One day, Mr. Sloan came to Dowdy to Daddy's store and said, "Mr. Coleman, I want you to cheer up. I'm going to make you a promise. If there's electricity turned on anywhere in this five-county area, it will be turned on in your house." They built four miles of line and gave my dad electricity when there wasn't another person in that four miles that would take it. Getting electricity meant there was a cord hanging from the ceiling with a light bulb, and a pull chain at the end of it.

Even then, people didn't want electricity in the area. They were skeptics and afraid of it. Some men took cross saws and sawed down the poles that carried electricity to our store. Sometimes, they would take their rifles and sever the lines by shooting them. Yes, they were good marksmen.

Within the next few years, though, everybody up and down the road had signed for electricity. Maybe the pleasure of listening to *Lum and Abner* on the radio at our store was the very thing that changed their minds.

My family always had a warm spot in our heart for Mr. Sloan. In addition to heading up the REA in that five-county area, he was also appointed to the State Highway Commission by Governor Homer Adkins. Mr. Sloan also served as Arkansas State Master of the Grange.

* * *

My dad was a pioneer in school consolidation. It took a lot of effort to persuade people in those little districts that consolidation was a good thing. They didn't like the idea of dismantling those one-room schools and consolidating them into bigger schools for the advantage of having a high school, junior high, and elementary grade school located in one place. Dad fought for consolidation really hard because he could see its benefits. My dad made a lot of enemies because of his progressive attitude toward school consolidation. Some people considered consolidation a "life and death" matter. They were so "sot" in their ways that they would nearly shoot one another over it. They were used to the way things were, and they wanted to keep it that way.

My folks always supported my brother, Van Doyne, my sister, Winona, and me in all of our school activities. My parents were members of the Grange and the 4-H Club. They took an active part in everything that was good and fostered leadership. They were charter members of the Independence County Historical Society.

The Strawberry School had all 12 grades, and was only 10 miles up the road from our house and five miles over the line into Lawrence County. There was a one-room school house on every little corner, including the Stone School House at Dowdy, Williams School House, Union School House, Hundred and Four, Hazel Grove, Walnut Grove, and Charlotte. Every little community had a one-room school that taught through the eighth grade and Strawberry School was just 10 miles up the road accommodating all 12 grades.

When I was 17 years old, I drove the school bus. I was a senior in high school. Every school day, my bus route was a

62-mile round trip. Dad and the Strawberry School Board asked a majority of patrons in the school district to sign a petition if they were willing for me to drive a school bus loaded with kids. I suppose their parents thought that I was mature enough to handle the situation. My dad didn't give me any money for driving the school bus, but I ate supper at home every night. Driving the bus was part of my day after I had been up at 4:00 in the morning milking the cows in the barn by a lantern light. I started milking cows when I was so small I had to stand up to reach the teats. I also fed the hogs before leaving for school. I wore the same shoes to school I wore to feed the hogs. That wasn't perfume you'd smell on them!

# My Second Toehold

My second toe hold came about because of my dad's honesty and hard work, and his relationship with Mr. J. M. Bryant. The J. M Bryant Company in Clarksville, Arkansas, was in the stave mill business. At one time Leslie Bryant, son of J. M. Bryant, was president of the American Cooperage Association, an association of all the stave mills in the United States that made white oak staves for whiskey barrels. That was big, big business. However, things didn't come easy for J. M. Bryant. As a young man, he was walking home one day after working in the timber there in Johnson County. He was tired and thirsty, so he stopped at a well and had to lean way over the well to get a drink. He got the drink, but then watched the only money he had in the world, a quarter, fall out of his pocket and spiral down to the bottom of the well.

The Dowdy post office was named for Mr. R. A. Dowdy because he owned a thousand acres of land down in the river bottoms. Mr. Dowdy was in the coal mining business at Clarksville, and he mortgaged the land down in the Black River Bottom to the J. M. Bryant Company in Clarksville. They took this land to settle the debt. So Mr. Bryant came to Charlotte, Arkansas, where the Weaver family owned a big stave mill. It was one of the biggest stave mills in the country at that time. My dad had always hauled timber, stave bolts, to Mr. Weaver up at Charlotte. Mr. Weaver always knew Daddy to be an honorable, hard-working, honest man.

(I don't know how the name got started, but a stave bolt had nothing to do with metal. A stave bolt is the piece of timber-plank that is steamed and pressurized to make it curve. Then it is joined with other staves to form a barrel.

Then metal bands are placed around the barrel to hold all the staves in place.)

One day Mr. Bryant came to Charlotte and said. "Mr. Weaver, we've bought staves from you all these years. We've got land down here on the Black River that I've never seen. I took it in on a debt. Could you recommend somebody who's honest to take care of that land and see that nobody steals my timber?" There was only one person in the world that would fit that category, and it was my dad. Mr. Weaver said, "I know a man that would be just perfect for that. Win Coleman."

Mr. Bryant came to see my dad, and Daddy agreed to do that. Mr. Bryant and Dad got to be good friends. Mr. Bryant would bring his family and their maid, and spend part of the summer at my parents' house. I was a young man at that time, and he and I got to knowing each other, and he liked me.

* * *

My dad used to cut timber, haul stave bolts, and haul cotton in the fall of the year—do anything to make a living with a truck. My mother and a hired man, Ben Blankenship, would plant the crop. Mother would take me to the field with her and put me on a blanket under a tree, and put a big rock on my dress tail to keep me from crawling off. While Mother and Ben were planting the crop, Dad was cutting timber.

I've seen my dad go for a week at a time and never take his shoes off. He would come in with a load of stave bolts on his truck, and my mother would get in that truck and drive it to Charlotte. The men up at Charlotte, at the stave mill, would unload the truck for her, and she would drive that empty truck back home. While she was gone, Dad would lie down on the floor and get a little sleep. Then when she got back with the truck, he would get up and go again.

In 1929, he bought a Model T Ford truck and began doing custom hauling. Dad had about the only truck in the area, and he would haul railroad cross ties that had been hewn from timber in nearby woods. These pieces of timber would weigh in excess of 300 to 400 pounds. My dad could go into the woods and put one of the timbers on his shoulder and walk out of the woods and put it on the truck by himself.

In those days Imboden, Arkansas, up in Lawrence County was where Dad had to take the cross ties to market. One day in 1930 when Dad was going to Imboden with a load, Melvin Prince, who had never been anywhere before, rode with Dad. While Dad was unloading the truck and settling up, Melvin went downtown. When Melvin came back to the truck, he said, "Mr. Coleman, a while ago I just bought one of the biggest oranges I ever saw. But you know that thing is so bitter I can't hardly eat it." Melvin had just had his first experience with a grapefruit.

Periodically, Dad would go into Batesville to get supplies for the store from the Wholesale Batesville Grocery Company owned by J. B. Kramer, and Arkansas Dry Good Store owned by the Barnett family. One time, Bennie Lance, an old bachelor who walked everywhere he went, rode into town with Dad. In town, he just walked up and down the street until Dad was ready to head home. When Bennie met back up with Dad, Bennie was outraged and flabbergasted. "Win, I just saw a woman in downtown Batesville with hardly no clothes on. Her skirt was so short, it was up to her you-know-what. The sheriff needs to get a hold of her. There ought to be a law against that." Bennie had just seen what was probably the first miniskirt worn in Batesville. He probably would have a heart attack if he were alive today and could see how people dress.

* * *

Mr. J. M. Bryant sold me my first thousand acres in 1945. I went to Clarksville to seal the deal, and I took Florene and

Carol Beth, who was just a tiny baby, with me. That was the first trip we had ever taken.

We went back home and started a sawmill. I went to cutting timber off that land with the intention of clearing the land and putting it into production. My dad, bless his heart, could not see that. He didn't mind my cutting timber, working in the timber business, but he thought that was the craziest thing he had ever heard of—to think about clearing that land and putting it into production as farmland. The day I began clearing land, my dad threw a fit with a hole in it. That's called a doozie.

He said, "You know, there ain't nobody ever done it, so what makes you think you can? If it could be done, some of the big shots from town would have already done it!" I said, "Well, Daddy, I ain't got nothing, and I don't mind working. I ain't got nothing to lose but my work, and I believe it will work."

With all due respect to my dad, he was honest in thinking that, but he was wrong in his thinking at that time. He really believed it could never be farmed because it was too swampy and too wet, and too risky, too many overflows. That's the only time I didn't listen to his advice. I started cutting that timber off, and now all of that land is in production with row crops. We sawmilled for 10 years. I was the sawyer, and I had a blocker and a log turner working with me. Some days, however, I had to do all three jobs at one time.

Fifty years later, my dad was right. It takes too long to grow the type of timber that was in that swamp. If I had that timber on that land today—the timber I cut, piled, and burned because I didn't know any better—would be worth twice as much now. Hindsight is always 20/20.

* * *

I started clearing section 13 (township 4 north, Range 3 west) beginning at the southwest corner of the north half where Turkey Hill Road turns north off Lockhart Road. I hired

Albert Lewellen to run an old stump saw to take down the trees. My brother, Van Doyne, helped clear using a stump saw. I paid him by the acre. I think I paid him around $20.00, but it takes a good operator to cut down an acre in one day.

Back then you could get land, timber and all, for $15.00 an acre. A pretty good standing bid for the timber was $10.00 an acre, and you would then let the owner have the land back for $5.00 an acre. So I cleared hundreds and hundreds of acres of land down there in the bottom. Nowadays people would say I was crazy for letting that land go for $5.00, but we didn't think the land was worth anything. I know it sounds crazy now, but it made sense then. I did buy back some of those acres, but not all. I could have owned 25,000 acres instead of 5,000, but I just didn't know any better.

When I started clearing land, it was still swamp and filled with so many cypress and other trees that were so big, they must have been there since the beginning of creation. Some were so big, nobody had anything big enough to cut them with. I knew a man in Paragould who had a really big dragline. It was big enough to carry and handle a cutter blade. With that you can drive right by a tree and cut it down as you go. The dragline was big enough it could carry the tree out onto the bank, and then bulldozers would come along and pile the timber in a heap to burn.

I put together a piece of land that we still call "over the levee" on Round Lake. I bought some of it from the Doc Stroud family in Jonesboro, some of it from the McGees, and 40 acres of it from Red Bell's father-in-law, Mr. Leanihan. I bought a little dab from Preston Grace. All the land was on the other side of the levee west of the river, and south of the mouth of the Strawberry River, about two thousand acres in all. The Old Lockhart School house was up there on a high piece of land just south of Round Lake.

In the 1950's just before I started clearing that land, they moved the old Lockhart School House from up there in the woods down to the river, down by that first little field as you went out to the Lockhart ferry. They placed it right there at that big red oak tree that was beside the road. That's where the old Lockhart School House was when it was torn down after being consolidated with the Cord District.

Before we started clearing, what land we had that could be farmed we planted in corn and sowed soybean seeds between the stalks of corn. After we had harvested the corn by hand, we would turn hogs loose in the soybeans and let them eat them. That way we had hogs fattened up for market.

Later we learned that soybeans could be a cash crop, but we still planted them between the stalks of corn. Instead of turning the hogs loose, we'd put a tarpaulin on the floor of the wagon and then run the wagon down the rows. We could take three rows at a time. We'd have one man on each side and one behind the wagon. If the rows were the right width, you could straddle a row and have a row on each side of the wagon. We'd pull the soybean plants up and warp them over the sideboards of the wagon so that the beans would fall onto the tarpaulin. Then after the soybeans were harvested, we'd stand up in the wagon and throw shovels of beans up into the air and hope for a good breeze. That's how we'd get the husk off the beans.

Then we would put the beans into tow sacks and take them over to the town of Diaz and sell them to Buck Hurley. That was my first experience with selling soybeans.

Finally combines came along. The first combine we ever saw belonged to Mr. Southerland down at Newark. It was an old Massey-Harris combine. We had a lot of good beans in the field that year, and we weren't going to put the hogs in there, so we got him to come up and thrash those beans with his combine. That was really some improvement from warping those buggers over the sideboards of a wagon. The combine had an auger that would unload clean beans into a truck bed to be hauled to market.

\* \* \*

Section 35, that's 640 acres, was for sale and everybody, including me, was trying to buy it. Section 35 was below Lockhart and below the house that Luther Melton built and painted green. That road is still called the Green House Road.

The man who owned it was a doctor's son in Palo Alto, California. I had written him trying to buy it, but I had never met the man. I had written him two or three times trying to negotiate a price, but then everybody was doing the same thing. I never could get the owner to give me a price.

So I thought about that for a while, and I decided the only way to make a deal is just to look a man right straight in the eye. So, I bought myself a plane ticket to California to look up the man and see if I could buy his land. I didn't want him to know that coming to see him was the only reason I was out there, so I fibbed and told him I was going to be in Palo Alto, say, next week on a certain day, and would he let me come by and talk to him about his land. He said, "Well, sure, come on by while you are out here, and see me about it."

There is no way to keep a secret in a small town. I had not told anyone about my plan to go to California. My dad walked in the day I bought the ticket and said, "I hear you are going to California next week." I was stunned. The man that sold me the plane ticket had called Charles Cole, a prominent lawyer in town and said, "Why is a country boy like Ewell Coleman, who has never been out of Independence County, going to California next week?" I have always said that the entire town knows who is pregnant by the next morning.

I landed in San Francisco and hired a taxi to take me to Palo Alto. I spent three days out there, but I came home with the deed to that land. I paid him $50.00 an acre for that land, and that was about $10.00 more than most people were offering, but it was a good buy. I think it was a good deal for him, and I know it was a good deal for me because it was loaded with timber. I cut the timber and sawmilled it, and I'm sure I got more money out of the timber than what I paid the man, and I cleared the land and put it into production.

I guess what that means is a little old farm boy with a pair of overalls was able to outdo the guys who already owned thousands of acres of land. Looking a man straight in the eye and offering a little bit more than the others who were competing for it did the trick.

* * *

The last thousand acres I bought belonged to Mr. M. D. Springfield who lived in Little Rock. Mr. Springfield died and didn't have any heirs, so again it was one of those cases where everybody wanted to buy it. Mr. Judson Hout and a lawyer named Bradley were named administrators of the Springfield estate.

I knew Mr. Hout really well, so I went to talk to him. This was in the 1960s. Mr. Hout was big in loaning money to buy land that was being cleared and developed in that region. He represented Kansas City Life, and if you had any kind of a deal at all, you could usually get it financed with Judson Hout. So I went down to his office in Newport. I told him I really wanted to buy that land because it joined the section I had just bought from the man in California. I will never forget what he said. "Now Monday morning, don't you go down there in no 'damned' suit of clothes. You go down there to Little Rock in a pair of overalls and a pair of work shoes. You tell Mr. Bradley that you are a dirt farmer." So I did. On

Monday morning I got up early and went to Little Rock to see Mr. Bradley the lawyer. I put on my overalls and a pair of work shoes. I was clean, but I did look like a dirt farmer. When I went into this big fine law office's reception lounge there in Little Rock, to my surprise there sat my brother, Van Doyne, in his best suit of clothes.

That was quite a contrast I'll never forget. There I was in my work clothes and my brother in his best suit of clothes. I said, "Well, good morning. I have an idea I know what you're here for. I know what I'm here for—to try to make a deal on that land. Since you were here first, go make your pitch first, and when you get through, I'll make mine."

Anyway, I was able to make the deal on the land. I don't know what kind of deal Van Doyne offered to Mr. Bradley. I didn't know anything about it. I don't know if the necktie threw him off, or if the overalls put me on. I just don't know which.

Another unique thing about that particular deal is that it was the last thousand acres I bought. Mr. Bradley was a lawyer who handled the deal. When I bought my first thousand acres from the J. M. Bryant Company at Clarksville, Mr. Bradley's brother, also a lawyer, had handled that deal.

That was one heck of year for me. I bought, cleared, planted, and harvested that thousand acres in that one year. Then I divided the land into thirds and gave each child of mine a third of that thousand acres.

* * *

In 1951 I went to Newark and bought a brand new d-5 bulldozer from Cecil Norris and hired Lester Harris to operate it. I went to cutting the timber and clearing that land. There was so much timber, we had to open a sawmill.

We had a fast sawmill and a power unit big enough to really saw lumber. I could take a good sized tie log, a couple of boards, and four stobs, and make a 7 X 9 crosstie in one minute. I could set the blocks, turn the log, and pull the handle to run the carriage all by myself in one minute. All the time it took to take a board off the log was the same amount of time it takes to say: zzzzzzip

Lefty Daggett was my log turner. Out of all the men who worked for me, Lefty was the stoutest man who ever turned logs for me. He could lay a cant hook in a log and nearly knock the carriage off its track when he turned the log.

No one had ever used a bulldozer to clear land in that area before. We put a lot of the early cleared land into rice. I drilled the first rice well in the county, and the first one on the west side of the Black River.

Back in the early days when I was very young—back in the mid 1920's and before that—this land was bad to overflow. There were big floods in 1913, 1915, and again in 1927, 1937, and 1945. Over the years since I cleared the land, the overflow hasn't been as bad. With all that big timber in that bottom, it didn't take much water to flood the land because the timber took up so much space. Now with the timber gone, we don't have floods like that. Take a bucket half full of water. Put a big rock in it. It will run over the top of the bucket. With the timber gone, the bucket isn't quite as full.

During one of the overflows, a Mr. Cecil Edgar Herring drowned, and they had to bury him on the only high piece of ground that was available. It was just below the mouth of the Strawberry River on the Black River portion. Junior Huskey owns that land now, but the grave has never been disturbed. We call it the graveyard field. The river is cutting away at the land there now and is only about 200 yards from the grave.

Another incident similar to that one happened once again in an overflow. Mr. Joe Inman, who worked at the Lockhart sawmill camp, tells the story about a man who died down at the camp. They had to bury his coffin in a large sawdust pile because it was the only thing that wasn't under water.

Later, I built the house we live in now. Florene and a hired hand did all the moving of what little stuff we had as I was out in the fields working. For about 10 years, we didn't have a stick of furniture in the living room. We had a big picture window, but there wasn't anything in the living room. I had taken what little money we had at the time and spent it on a brand new Allis-Chalmer bulldozer. My dad said, "Florene, if I was you, I'd go get that bulldozer, and I'd drive it right through that front window and park that bulldozer in the living room, or make him buy you some furniture to go in there." I thought buying the bulldozer was a better use of money for the family than living room furniture. Right or wrong, that's what I did.

As I look back on life, I tried to do a lot of things that I thought were progressive for the community and improving the river bottom, which at one time was just swamp. It had to be cleared; it had to be drained; it needed to be put into production. You can't raise a corn patch or a bean patch in a mud hole.

I knew that, and I thought everyone else did, too—that the better drainage we had, the better off everybody would be. I've fought all my life trying to get some good drainage down in the bottom, but I could never get it done. At that time, I was on the Soil Conservation District Board and on the State Board. I was in a lot of places with people who had influence and leadership that could have got a lot of things done. But some of the local people petitioned against and wouldn't accept it. They just would not cooperate with me and the federal agencies and other people who could get it done. They just could not see it.

\* \* \*

In 1915, the federal government came in here and built what we called the Curie Creek ditches. They rerouted the creek due east into the river at Horseshoe Lake and ran it into Horseshoe Lake. The lake runs into the river just a quarter mile or so below the mouth of the Strawberry River. Buzz Martz told me that when the government built the Curie Creek ditches, they brought in "colored" people and had them housed in a tent. The workers were batching up here, cooking and eating and sleeping in the tent. One night some people went up there and cut the tent down with those people inside lying in bed and ran them off.

Another time, a man from Carlisle came into here and brought 15 or 20 black laborers to cut timber and run the sawmill. Some of the white people just weren't going to allow it, and it wasn't but just a few days until there wasn't a black man left in the community. So then the man had to come back and bring in a white crew from down around Carlisle to cut timber and run the sawmill. Some of those men ended up staying in the community and made it their home. Tood Wilson and a man named Anderson were two who stayed to raise families at Cord.

* * *

We were trying to form a Drainage District to clean out Currie Creek, and the man from Paragould with the dragline made me a bid of $100,000 to clean Currie Creek from Turkey Hill Road down to where it runs into the river just below Elgin.

That scared some people completely to death. Some who would have benefitted the most from it would have to pay more taxes. It would be paid for by placing an assessment on the land for the drainage. I thought this would have been one of the best things that ever happened to this community, but I couldn't get everybody to see it. Some of them fought me like a tiger on that, and wouldn't do it—though it would have cost less than $2.00 an acre to have done that. And now it's still hard to a raise crop down there because the dadgum beavers have got the creek stopped up, and there's just no drainage down there. It was just like it was when we were trying to get electricity into the area.

The same was true with getting telephone service into the area. We were trying to do business at Dowdy, and if we wanted to make telephone calls concerning business, or anything else, we had to go to Cord to make the call. I was brokering 200,000 bushels of soybeans for Riceland Food, which meant I was running back and forth to Cord several times a day to use the pay phone. You can imagine how inconvenient that was.

I worked and worked and worked to try to get a telephone line from Cord to Dowdy. The telephone company wanted a certain number of subscribers to the mile before they would put in the line. As hard as I tried to get people to subscribe for phone service, I was unsuccessful. Too many people from Cord to Dowdy would not sign up for telephones, and I needed telephone service so badly that I finally diverted my farm crew from clearing land for crops and had them clear the right of way for the telephone line.

We cut timber, we cut brush, we cut small trees—whatever had to be done for that telephone line. Then I paid to get the line put in, and I paid for those people's telephone bill for the first year. That way I knew that if they had a telephone for just one year, they would never have them taken out of their houses, so that's the way we got telephones to Dowdy.

One thing I have learned and have observed during my lifetime is that we human beings are pretty much set in our ways, and it takes a lot of persuasion to change our attitudes about things. It takes a lot of persuasion, and change comes about by much pain and time and education. We don't learn things too fast. It has to come slowly, and what we believe, we really believe. And it is hard to change a person when he thinks a certain way. I have lived when there was no electricity and now the world runs on electricity. No progress comes easily.

\* \* \*

The years went by! The 1940s turned into the 1950s. We bought land, cut timber, sawmilled for 10 years in the 1940s. We sawmilled for 10 straight years. Then in the 1950's we cleared land for 10 years straight and put it into production. The last thousand acres of land we cleared and put into production was in 1963. We cleared that land all in one year, and disked it up and put it into production—all in one year. That took some doing!

During the time I was doing all this clearing and all this farming, Florene would take the kids and catch a truck here in front of the house that was on the route driven by Gaynell Gipson. They would ride the truck across the river at Lockhart and on over into Jackson County and pick cotton.

We all worked, and everybody had his part to play to help build up the family. We were working every day, and we had lots of things going with all the kids at home. The Lord blessed me, and we were able to send all three children to college. All three are college graduates and are successful in their professions.

Just to show you how honest and innocent Florene was, I had a seine that we used to catch fish with—and yes, it was illegal to do that. It had a one-inch mesh, which made it illegal. You could take that seine and easily catch some perch. Homer Brewer had got mad at me for some reason, so he went and told the game warden about me and my seine. I wasn't any real lawbreaker. I would just seine us a mess of fish once or twice a year. Mr. Brewer said that I had a 30-foot seine at my place, which was illegal.

One evening as the kids and Florene were coming in from picking cotton, the game wardens were there to meet them. It scared Florene to death to see them there with their guns on their sides and the whole bit. They told her they had been told I had a seine, but they didn't tell her it was illegal. They just said they wanted to see it. Florene took them all over the place trying to help them find that seine. Just a day or two before, I had taken it off the back fence where it usually stayed and had put it in the barn. They never did find the seine, and that was the end of that. I guess if they had found it, they would have put me in jail. We'll never know.

During those years while Donald was in college, we were farming big. I was farming 5,000 acres of land at that time with a bunch of old G-John Deere tractors. Those old two-cylinder tractors and a bunch of old Amco disks were what we used to disk up all this new ground. One of things I think you will find is that everybody who ever worked for me will tell you I am a hard worker. They might not have liked it—because I worked my crews hard—but you'll never find anybody who won't admit that I never asked anyone to do something I wouldn't do myself, or already had, before I would ask anyone else to do it. My thinking is that if I can do a whole lot of a certain thing, then I want you to try to do a little of it.

# My Third Toehold

The third toehold in my life was my marrying Lois Florene Hugg, my high school sweetheart. Florene was the youngest daughter of Allie Lou Gardner Williams and William "Will" Baxter Hugg. Florene was born at Strawberry, Arkansas, and lived there her entire life until we married in 1944.

Her father's first wife died leaving him with two children, Floyd and Ollie Hugg. Mr. Hugg then married Mrs. Allie Gardner Williams who was a widow and had a son, Gardner Williams. Will and Allie had three children, Kenneth, Kathleen, and Florene.

Mr. Hugg raised his family on a small, hill farm. He farmed cotton, reared a few cattle and hogs, and then cut wood to sell in the winter.

Florene was born and reared in a three-room log house with an open hallway "dog trot" between the rooms. There was a fireplace at the end of each room that provided heat, and a wood cook stove in the kitchen area for preparation of food. They drew water from a well located at the corner of the yard. They never had electric lights or indoor plumbing, and walked everywhere they went. The Huggs lived approximately one to two miles from Strawberry, school, and church.

Mrs. Hugg was in the church house every time the door was open. Day or night, she walked about two miles to church and back home and carried a kerosene lantern at night. Miss Allie, the name everybody called her, was always proud to say, "I'm a Baptist and a Democrat."

Mr. Hugg was known to take a drink of whiskey once in a while. He would walk across the field to one of the neighbors who made moonshine whiskey and wine. Mr. Hugg would buy some blackberry or grape wine. He'd bring it home and hide it at the barn in the corn crib. Sometimes, Miss Allie would find it and break the bottles over the logs; that would stop his nipping for a while. However, it didn't stop it for long, and the tug of war would start all over again.

Florene attended what we call Strawberry High School, but it started as Strawberry Academy, a tuition school. One year, she had to drop out of school because her father hadn't cut enough wood to pay her tuition. Florene had to walk two miles each way, everyday, to go to school. She did her homework by kerosene lamp. During her senior year, she worked in the school library for a little income. She finished high school as valedictorian of her senior class.

That was during World War II, and teachers were scarce. If an individual could pass a county supervisor's test, they were issued a certificate to teach. Passing that test was no problem for Florene! She and her friend Norma Louise Williams taught school at Rich Woods for two years before we married.

As a result of her teaching experience, she has always said, "I brought $290 into this marriage which matched the $200 you had saved from selling a few hogs and cattle. So we started out almost even and have been partners ever since."

We didn't have much in the way of material possessions. I had a shirt, a pair of pants, and shoes, and she owned a dress and a pair of shoes. I also owned a wagon with iron wheels and a pair of $50 mules. I had made a little money farming. That's how we started out. My dad said, "Ewell, you ain't got nothing, but if you will be honest, you will make it."

We had had a pretty exciting courtship, however. I was at Florene's house one night. She and I were in the room across the dog trot from the living/kitchen room. I struck a match on the window screen in order to light a kerosene lamp. As I pulled that match back through the curtains, they caught on fire. I yanked off those curtains, ran out into the yard, and started stomping on them. Mr. Hugg came running out there wanting to know what was going on. I could have burned down the house trying to light that kerosene lamp. What a frightening and embarrassing incident!

Florene was a smart, good looking young lady. Most importantly, she was a Christian. I was looking for a good woman, and I found her in Florene. I thought a mother had more influence on the family than the father. Back then, a mother raised the children, and the father made the living for the family. A mother usually spent twice as much time with the children as did their father. I knew I could make a living, and that I could work. I felt a responsibility to provide for my wife, my family, and our home.

Florene and I got married on a Saturday night, April 22, 1944. I will never forget the rainstorm we had that night. You can't believe how hard it rained! We were married by a Justice of the Peace, Bye Andrews. Mr. Andrews lived way back, a half mile or more, down a muddy lane east of Strawberry. We had to walk down that lane in the rain because driving was impossible.

Florene wore a crepe dress and borrowed a coat from her sister, Kathleen. Everybody knows what happens to crepe fabric when it gets wet... it shrinks. I chuckle when I say that mini-skirts started the night we got married. As we walked down to Bye Andrews' house to get married, the front of Florene's dress got wet, and it shrunk way above her knees.

The new coat Florene borrowed from Kathleen got wet, too. She took off the coat, and draped it over an old iron, cane bottom chair Mr. Andrews had sitting on the front porch. The iron metal rusted on Kathleen's brand new coat. Florene was so upset and couldn't believe she had damaged Kathleen's coat. That rusty stain never came out.

After the marriage ceremony, we planned to go to Cave City to the movies with our friends Aldean Milligan and Bill Penn. We got about halfway between Strawberry and Cave City. It was raining and storming so badly, we had to turn around and go back to Strawberry.

We spent our honeymoon night at Florene's parents' house. That was on a Saturday night, and the next day on Sunday afternoon, duty called us back to Dowdy. After a rain like that, the river was bound to overflow our farmland. We had to go to Black River bottoms and retrieve farm equipment that would likely get covered with floodwater.

Florene and I lived with my parents for about six months after we married. We later moved into a four-room house we called the "old black house" which was in the yard adjacent to my parents' house and their country store complex. I guess we called it the "black house" because the boards on the outside were grey and black, weather-beaten boards. We could see the stars through holes in the roof and feed chickens through crevices in the floor. Seven years later, in 1951, I was able to build for us a large, stone house where we lived until the spring of 2005. Florene became seriously ill, and we moved to Little Rock to be near our daughters and needed medical facilities.

No man could ask for a better wife than Florene. She was always a very patient woman and sacrificed much so that the family might succeed. She was a wonderful cook. She enjoyed gardening. Florene canned and stored much of our food for the winter. She liked to sew and made most of the dresses and clothes for our two daughters.

Florene was an active member in the Baptist Church her entire life. She taught every grade in Sunday school, plus participated in many other church activities. We took the children to church—we didn't just send them to church. I also taught Sunday school and was a deacon in the church. I was the Sunday school superintendent at both Cord and Dowdy churches.

* * *

Florene died February 12, 2007, and was buried on February 16 at the Hopewell Cemetery with the rest of the Coleman and Winston families.

At her funeral, Clemon Williams, a relative and friend from Strawberry, told a story about her when they were in high school at Strawberry. One of their classmates became severely ill and was bedridden for a long period of time. Every afternoon after school, Florene would walk to his house to take him homework assignments and tutor him. She tutored him with his school work throughout his illness, and he was able to pass that grade.

# On the Way up the Mountain

People made a living any way they could. They either raised a few cattle and hogs, worked in the timber, raised cotton on any little patch of land they could find, or made moonshine whiskey. They grew what they ate, and about all they would need money for was to buy a little baking powder, coffee, and sugar.

People in the hills would run their livestock in what they called free range. The cattle could graze down in the river bottom on cane, switch cane, and swamp grass, and thrive really well. Folks would also run their hogs in the bottoms. Back then, there were hickory nuts, acorns, and all kinds of wild plants that the animals could eat. They would run the livestock down there in the summer time and take them out in the fall, and the livestock would be fat.

Mr. Oder Birmingham was a prominent man here in the community, and he always had a lot of cattle and a lot of hogs. He ran them down in the bottom at free range. When an overflow would come, which was quite often, he would have to go down to the bottoms and round up the hogs and put some of them in a boat and drive the rest out of the bottoms.

Just north of Lockhart, the Black River made a really sharp bend and went about a half a mile or more back east, and then came back nearly to where it started just below the mouth of the Strawberry River. It was known as Purcell Bend. The river kept trying to cut through there. There was sort of a low place on the back bone, and Mr. Birmingham would have trouble with his cattle getting back there on that high ridge when the river would get up a little bit, and he couldn't get them out of there.

He got tired of that and decided to do something about it. He had a dynamite auger, and I would borrow it from him every once in a while to dynamite a stump. One day when I went over to borrow the auger, Mr. Birmingham said, "Ewell, right here is the auger that turned the Black River." I had heard him say that many times.

One time when an overflow had started, he took the auger over to that high ridge where the river was trying to cut through and dynamited it. When the river went down, the river was just as wide right in that spot as it was everywhere else. The river had flowed right through there because Mr. Birmingham had loosened all that dirt with the dynamite. The river would have eventually cut through there, but Mr. Birmingham gave it a boost.

There is a nice big farm on that land now, but we still call it Purcell Bend.

* * *

One day, a man came into Dad's store and said, "Win, I don't know what I am going to do. I put up eight hogs in the smokehouse and six tow sacks full of peas and beans, and someone has stolen all of it. That's how I planned to feed my family this winter." Dad tried to comfort him. There was a family in the neighborhood that was suspected of thieving. Everybody was pretty sure who was doing the thieving, but couldn't catch them red-handed—until one night when one of the daughters in the suspected family invited a school chum over for supper. That night, the main dish was sows' ears. The school friend immediately recognized the markings on the sows' ears to be those of her Dad's hogs. Farmers registered the markings on their hogs' ears at the courthouse so there was no question as to who the hogs had belonged. Dad's friend, who had had his hogs stolen, wanted something done, but didn't have the money to prosecute. Plus he was afraid they would harm his family and burn down his house. Dad said that if they were going to continue to live in that place, then things like that had to stop. Dad told his friend that if he would sign the papers to prosecute, Dad would put up the money. The head of the house got arrested and was sent to the penitentiary. The moral of that true story is if you are going to invite guests for dinner, don't serve them stolen food.

\* \* \*

I heard my dad talk about the old Miller field which was east of Cord just down under the foothills toward the Elgin Ferry. He said it was the best place in the world to cut swamp grass hay. The folks would go down there and cut the swamp grass hay, and then put the hay up to feed the livestock in the winter time.

Across the county line in Jackson County, the land was sandy and most all of it was in production. Folks from the hills would go over there in the fall and pick cotton and make a little money. During my school days, school would be let out four to six weeks in the fall so the kids could go with their parents to pick cotton. They picked cotton not only in Jackson County, but also around Leachville, in Mississippi County. When the cotton was all picked, they would come back across the bottoms and go back up into the hills and live on that money during the winter.

The only steady money that could be made was by working in the timber, or by working at the sawmill, cutting bolts or cutting white oak staves. That was a thriving business. White oak makes the best staves, and we had a lot of timber in the area. The basic need for white oak staves was to make whiskey barrels. It took good timber to make white oak staves that would hold whiskey.

Bartering was also a way of life. Local people would bring chickens and eggs to the grocery store and trade them for groceries. Robert Stroud and his father ran a paper route and an egg route out to our area. Robert Stroud's father-in-law, Dee Lester, gave me my first start in the banking business. He sold me a few shares at first and then later sold me enough shares that I could sit on the board.

The other big business in that area was making moonshine whiskey. I've heard my Dad say that when he was a young boy, there weren't enough men left in Cord to put out a fire because they were all in the jail at Batesville for making moonshine whiskey. Allie Warren, a native of Cord, says it was actually 30 men who were in jail. Her father was chairman of the Grand Jury that indicted them, and Adrain Long escorted her father home that night with a shot gun.

There was a piece of land in the Black River bottoms known as Crews Bend. Buzz Martz remembers that when he was a young man, there were 14 stills in that one river bend. Making moonshine whiskey was big business in the 1920s. The moonshiners would load their barrels of whiskey on boats and send them down the Black River to Jacksonport where the Black empties into the White River. From there the barrels went down the White to the Mississippi River and then upstream to St. Louis.

I have never had a drink of whiskey in my life, but I want to tell you that just because those people made moonshine whiskey, they weren't bad people. That just happened to be the way they made a living. Some of the finest people in the world, that treated you right, did you right, whose word was their bond, were the people who made moonshine whiskey. In the 1950s I cleared the land at Crews Bend and found the old steel staves off the barrels where they make their mash, the old brick fireplaces, and old pots. What was left of four or five whiskey stills remained at that time.

* * *

In the 1940s, I bought what was known as the Miller land. There were two pieces to that property. One was 120 acres west of Currie Creek, which is about a mile from the river and about a mile from the Miller land where Daddy cut the hay. There was another 160 acres of land also up on Salt Work Slough. I bought both pieces of land from Mrs. Miller, the heir of the Dr. Miller family who came into that area before the Civil War. She was elderly at the time I purchased it.

I cleared that land and put it into row crop production. Now that land is precision leveled, and we raise soybeans and rice on that acreage every year. We have underground irrigation pumps to pump water out of the underground aquifer or the river. Our pumps will produce about 1,500 gallons of water per minute to flood the rice. The aquifer there is 80 feet deep. Our river pumps will pump 10,000 gallons per minute.

Earlier when we were starting to really put in big crops of soybeans, we nearly lost it all. One fall we had a really big crop of soybeans ready to harvest. The beans were mature and ready to cut, and here came an overflow that covered the bottom up plus the beans. Those beans were 99 percent of everything we were trying to raise down there. But we didn't lose that crop. We were able to salvage a big end of it. The water went down and the beans dried out. The soybean is inside an oily shell, so that saved them. They dried out and we harvested that crop; however, the plants and beans were covered with mud. When we started combining them, all the dirt would fly out of the back of the combine. You couldn't even see the combine. All you could see was a brown cloud moving across the field.

We made just about as much out of that crop as we would have ordinarily, because that flood wasn't just here, but it was most everywhere else. That sent the price of soybeans up. The price offset the reduced yields, and that price increase is what bailed us out. I have often said that I am just one overflow away from bankruptcy.

In the '60s, we were farming big, so we put up a grain elevator and some storage bins, and bought soybeans from surrounding farmers. We were the agent for Riceland Foods. We weighed the beans, graded the beans, stored them, moved them from here at Dowdy to Newark, put them on a boxcar, and shipped them mostly to Helena, but some to Stuttgart. We averaged handling 250,000 bushels of beans a year.

Joe Kennedy, a neighbor, ran the elevator for me. He not only weighed and graded the beans, he kept up with the number of bushels we took in. We paid the farmers a fair price right then. We wrote them checks on the Riceland Foods' bank account. The farmers didn't make all that much money, but it gave the people here a good outlet for their soybeans, and they didn't have to haul them but a few miles out of the river bottom up here to the elevator.

Back then, we didn't have very good roads. The roads from Dowdy to Newark and the railroad were gravel. I remember one day that I had Jerry Turner from Strawberry driving my truck. We would load the beans here on a truck and haul them to Newark where there was a large grain elevator. I had a loading facility where we could dump the trucks and run the beans over into a boxcar. In that one 24-hour period, Jerry had nine flats on a tandem truck hauling beans. One of the tires picked up a horse shoe and, of course, the tire went flat. Some people were still using wagons and teams, and there were horse shoes, nails, and everything you could imagine on the road that could cause a flat. It wasn't because we didn't have good tires. It was just because of the conditions of the roads.

The Highway Department would run a magnetic truck over the roads to pick up the metal so you could run pneumatic tires up and down the road without having a flat every few miles.

* * *

During the time we were buying soybeans, a snake bit me. One fall, we were getting right ready to start into the soybean harvest, and one morning we were all ready to go to the fields. No beans had been cut yet, and we hadn't cleaned out the elevator pit so we could start loading into the tanks. Some leaves had blown across the grill of the elevator pit where we dumped the trucks. That pit would hold a truckload of beans. It was about eight or 10 feet deep, and the walls were slanted so that the beans would all go down to one point to go into the elevator. Everybody had gone to the fields but me, and I thought I had better run out there and get those leaves before somebody started that elevator with them in there and stopped up all the pipes.

I got a tow sack and proceeded to go out there and get those leaves out. So I set a ladder down into that pit and crawled down in there and began to get those leaves, picking them up with my hands and putting them into the sack so I could throw them out. All of a sudden I felt a sting on the back of my right index finger. It felt like a wasp sting. I looked around to see where the wasp nest was, but I didn't see any. I then looked down and there was a copperhead snake right down between my feet there in those leaves. So I knew at that moment I was snake bit. My first thought was that I had on a pair of leather hightop boots that came up above my ankles. I thought, well, boy, I'll just stomp your head off. Then I thought, well, you will bite me on the leg so I better get out of here and leave you alone.

So I did. I crawled out, and the first thing I did was to put that finger in my mouth and started sucking on the spot where the snake had hit me. Then I spit out as much as I could. I went to the house and told Florene, who sort of went into a little tizzy. It just felt like a wasp sting and nothing else. Florene insisted I go to the doctor. I protested, but I did go into Batesville to see Dr. Ketz. The first thing they ask you when you go to the doctor with a snake bite was what kind of snake it was. I told him it was a copperhead. He asked if I was sure. I said, "Well, it was a copperhead, and as many of those things as I've seen, I'm sure that was a copperhead."

Dr. Ketz went to the drugstore and got some anti-venom copperhead medicine and came back and gave me a shot. Over a period of time that morning, I had three shots. But by the middle of the afternoon it wasn't long until my arm began to swell up about three or four inches in diameter, and it just went up my arm. The swelling in my arm went on up to my neck. My neck just leveled out between my chin and my neck, plus there was a big old pone down my back. By the middle of the afternoon I wasn't in too good a shape. I just kept on going. It didn't make me sick; I just felt woozy. I've seen plenty of people drunk, and that's how I felt. I was just sort of loopy-legged.

That went on for several days, and it finally climaxed. My hand just nearly sloughed off. When the doctor dressed my hand, he would just pull off big flakes of flesh. My hand got well, and I kind of got over that, but not completely. The tenth day after I was bitten, about 3:00 one Monday morning, I woke and, man, I was hurting and I was sore, every inch of flesh on my body so painful I couldn't stand for anything to touch it. But it was a Monday morning when everything had to be organized for the work crew. At that time, we had assembled about 10,000 bushels of beans that had to be moved to Newark.

Since Jerry Turner had just started working for me, I hadn't had time to teach him how to seal the boxcars once they were loaded. I knew I had to go with him to Newark and show him how to fill out a bill of lading and everything else that goes with shipping beans.

I told Florene that if I wasn't better when daylight came, and if I didn't feel any better than I felt right then, I'd never be able to get off that bed. By daylight, I was a little better, so I got out of bed, but I wasn't too sporty. I went on to work and got everybody started and went with Jerry to Newark and showed him how to nail a boxcar door up so that he could load the beans.

By 10:00, I was out of it. I just couldn't go any farther. So they hauled me to the doctor in an ambulance. I was as stiff as a board. And every joint in my body just froze up, even my jaws. I couldn't even work my mouth.

They took me to the hospital, and Dr. Ketz came right over and my dad and Florene were there. My dad insisted that Dr. Ketz send me to Little Rock. "That boy is in bad shape!" Dr. Ketz didn't want to do that, and he said, "Win, I tell you what let's do. I believe I can curb this, so let's keep him here 24 hours, and if he's not progressing, then I'll agree to send him to Little Rock. Dr. Ketz began to doctoring me, and I was a little better the next morning. I stayed in the hospital for 10 days , and I don't believe I ever took as much medicine in my life. The nurses were giving me a shot every little bit, and I had IVs running in both arms, and I had to swallow a pill every few minutes.

I got over it and the day came when I was ready to go home. I was in Gray's Hospital in Batesville, and it was run by Mrs. Gray. When I went downstairs to settle up the bill, she started figuring it up. She looked up at me and said, "My God, son, did they give you this much medicine?" She said that there wasn't anybody who could take that much medicine no longer than I have been in there. I said, "Well, I don't know,

Mrs. Gray. All I know is that I have an idea the nurse kept up with it pretty good." I told her what all and how often I had been given medicine. She was sure no one could take that much medicine in that short of a time. It didn't seem like a short period of time to me. She said she would go back over the bill and if there was a mistake she would let me know.

That afternoon she called, and there had been a mistake. The bill was several hundred dollars higher than she first had figured. But I am alive today. The only aftermath of the snake bite is that my right index finger is sort of crooked.

In this area, a copperhead, a cottonmouth, and a rattlesnake will kill you more times as not. And those are the only three snakes we've got here that are really life-threatening. Some other snakes, those old water snakes and water moccasins will swell you up, and maybe make you sick, but they won't kill you.

There were only two other times I was in the hospital. On a routine medical check-up, the doctor discovered I had colon cancer. After exploring M. D. Anderson and the Mayo Clinic, I discovered that one of the best colon surgeons was right here in Batesville, Arkansas. Dr. John Lambert removed eight inches of my colon. The surgery was extremely successful, and I am completely free of cancer.

In 1998, I realized I was getting really short of breath, so once again I consulted a doctor, and it was a good thing I did. Tests showed that I had five blocked or partially blocked heart arteries. I underwent open-heart surgery at Baptist Hospital in Little Rock. Dr. John M. Ransom, who was reared at Pleasant Plains, not 20 miles from Cord, performed the operation. The hardest part of the surgery, for me, was the fact I had to behave myself physically for six weeks. I am not used to inactivity. Current tests show no heart blockage at all. Being in the hospital only three times in 82 years is a pretty good record.

# The Top of the Mountain

We were going along in the 1960s and early '70s, putting land into production. I had expanded into the certified soybean seed business. I shipped soybeans, from these 5,000 acres we farmed, all over this country and exported beans and seed beans to Mexico. I built a seed plant, storage buildings, and everything to handle and process seed soybeans. During that time, we were farming big, and I made a little money.

Tom Vinson was my banker in Batesville, and the only banker I had ever known personally until I bought the First National Bank in Batesville. Back in my hey-days was when Tom Vinson first began in banking, and back in the days when we were doing all this buying and clearing of land and so on, I made my first long-term loan with Travelers Life Insurance Company with the help of Tom. It was a loan of a million dollars and represented a first for me and Gordon Cox, the Travelers's loan officer who was also a farm boy. That was the first loan Gordon had ever made for Travelers, and it was the first time in my life to borrow a million dollars. This was pretty big stuff for two country boys. When Mr. Cox retired, years later he was the office manager for the southeastern U.S. office for Travelers Life Insurance Company in Atlanta, Georgia.

Tom had a lot of confidence in me, and he knew I would do whatever I said I would. Tom always kept an open banknote for me. I'd go by the bank, and he'd say, "Ewell, you need to sign some more notes, I am about to run out." He always loaned me all the money I've ever used all those years on an open note. He never asked me to mortgage anything. I could go any place, be it Memphis or New York or wherever, and I could write a pretty good-sized check, and I knew it wouldn't bounce because when that check came to the bank, Tom would run one of those notes in and cover it. Tom also knew I wouldn't write a check unless I knew it was okay.

Nowadays, you aren't allowed to do business that way; it would be illegal. Now they would make you sign a piece of paper a mile long in a dozen places, and you'd have to have a pick-sack to carry the paperwork home.

* * *

I got into the banking business to start with through Dee Lester. Mr. Lester had a corn sheller over at Desha. If you had any corn to sell, that's where you would go. We hauled our corn over to Mr. Lester's, and we got to know each other really well. Mr. Lester sold me the first bank stock I ever owned. It was stock in the First National Bank at Batesville. Later, Mr. Lester sold me enough bank stock to put me on the board of that bank. I served on the board of First National Bank for about three years until I bought the bank. That was in the early '70s.

During that time, while I was on the board, two of the largest stockholders got to logger-heading pretty good, and the bank was going downhill. Those two men couldn't get along, and it was hurting the bank. Both men were smart in their own way, but they couldn't agree to open a window or not if it came up for a vote.

I started talking to both of those men about my buying the bank. Try as we might, we could never agree on how to do it. There wasn't a way in the world that Jesus Christ himself could have bought that bank and let them stay on as owners. I tried to buy each man's bank stock; we worked on that deal back and forth for several years. That never worked out, either.

I had $750,000 in a bank in Memphis, so I just decided to buy the bank myself. That was a pretty big talk for a little country boy, but I didn't know any better, I guess. By that time, Tom Vinson was disgusted with all of us and quit and went up the street to Citizens Bank.

At the time I was dealing with Worthen Bank in Little Rock about buying out the stock holdings of those two men, I didn't have any better sense to make the deal without knowing whether Worthen would finance all of it. I went to Little Rock and talked to Ed Penick about the sale. Mr. Penick had more history on First National in Batesville than anyone in the state because several other people had been trying to buy the bank and finance it through Worthen. I hadn't known about that. As it turned out since they already had all the information on the bank, they were more than happy to be a part of buying the bank, if Mr. Penick approved the transaction. The problem was that Mr. Penick was out of the country on vacation and had left word he did not want to be reached—period! That left me in a bind because the board had given me one week to make the deal.

I talked to Larry Brashears at Worthen. I told him that I didn't need Mr. Penick right that minute but I would probably need him later. I had enough money to make a down payment on the bank. I knew it might be a mistake. I knew it might mean that I would have to scrape up some money somewhere to make a crop the next year; I even said I might have to rob a bank, but I wanted that deal nailed down right then. So I did it. I took every dime I had, not knowing if I could get it financed.

J. O. Michelle was my accountant, and we fixed up the paperwork. We put part of it in E. R. Coleman Farms and part of it in my individual name. At that particular time, we put too much of the ownership of the bank in E. R. Coleman Farms, which the government claimed was a holding company. J. O. Michelle argued with them on that, but they made us redo the ownership of the bank to where it finally wound up the other way around. J. O. finally said I was better off to do it that way money-wise and tax-wise. So that's another example of how the laws will sometimes, you know, strain at a gnat and swallow a camel.

On a Friday afternoon, I went to Little Rock and told Larry Brashears just "to forget it." I would finance it myself. On Sunday night about midnight, the phone rang and it was Ed Penick. Ed said, "Ewell, looks like you made yourself a good deal." I said, "Well, I don't know whether I made myself a good deal or not." He said, "I'm sorry that I was out of pocket here for the last 10 days, but I just do that about once a year. I just go off somewhere to where nobody can find me." I told him, "Well. Boy, they couldn't and, man, they really tried." I even accused them of faking the whole thing that he was in an undisclosed location. I guess he really was.

Ed asked, "What can I do for you? Come on down in the morning, and we will fix up the paperwork and you'll get your money on that bank." I said, "Ed, let's just think about that just for a little bit. Let me study about that." I knew that Worthen had been a corresponding bank for First National for years, and I thought they had done a good job, but I didn't know exactly what that job entailed. Being a country boy and not knowing any better, I told him, "I needed you real bad last week, but I don't need you right now. I knew that $750,000 would give me control of the bank for a year, but I didn't know where the other three million was coming from.

I told Mr. Penick what I was willing to do. I was willing to go into this partnership with Worthen and let them continue to be our corresponding bank, but first, I wanted a relationship with him. I just wanted to know that whatever it was they did for us didn't include ripping us off. I didn't mean to be disrespectful, but if I could get that done cheaper somewhere else, that was what I was going to do.

Oh, boy, he started begging me, "Now don't you do that. I want to continue to serve that bank." In other words, what he really was saying was "write your own ticket." We went with Worthen, and it was a good deal.

\* \* \*

At the time I bought the bank, I didn't know anything about banking. I knew the basic principles of the business, but as far as the inside details, the day-to-day activities inside the bank and what it took to run it, I didn't have a clue. I subscribe to the Henry Ford theory. Henry Ford said, "I can't build a car, but I can hire some people that can." I knew that I had to get a good banker and that he and I could work together. A man that could run the bank like I ran the farm.

I proceeded to try to find such a man. I wanted a man who was honest and had integrity, but also could stir things up and get the bank back to moving in the right direction. I sought out Lex Golden, Mayor Peyton Golden's boy, who was an officer in one of the Little Rock banks and was head of the traveling correspondent banks. As part of his job he had traveled all over the state, and he knew every banker in Arkansas.

I asked Lex if he knew a banker who would be willing to come to Batesville and run this bank and do what I wanted done. He thought about it for a while and then said, "Ewell, there's a banker at Jacksonville, and I think he's just the man you are looking for. His name is Mickey Twyford." Mickey was raised at Newport and is a real go-getter and had been a loan officer at Newport. He had owned the bank at DeLight, Arkansas, but had sold it and gone to work for Harold Gwatney at First National in Jacksonville. Mickey was kind of like me in that he had come up the hard way and had some farming background.

I visited with him several times and decided he was just the kind of man I wanted as bank president. At the bank in Jacksonville, he said he was making $27,000 a year, and if I would raise his salary to $37,000 a year, he would come to Batesville. I thought that was an outrageous request!

I asked Bill Bowen, who was then the President of First Commercial Bank in Little Rock, what he thought about the $37,000 figure. Bill said that was too much. I told Mickey what Mr. Bowen had said. Mickey's reply was, "I thought I was going to be working for you and not Mr. Bowen." Mickey's wife, Marcy, saved the day by saying "Mr. Coleman, you won't just be getting Mickey; you'll be getting me, too. It's two for the price of one. I'll work just as hard as Mickey to build up that bank." And she did, too. Instead of hiring one person, I got two for one salary, just as she said.

However, everything didn't go smoothly. I brought Mickey up to Batesville and called a board meeting, and you know what? My board turned him down! They just fuzzed him up, questioned him, and made him feel little, and when they got ready to vote, they asked Mickey to leave the room. They let a man of his caliber sit outside for over an hour. Mickey went home that night not knowing if he had a job, after my bringing him in there. I thought he was the best man I could find, and he was.

The next morning, I called Mickey, and he said, "Mr. Coleman, I'm not going to come!" In other words, what he was saying was that regardless of what he was offered, he was not coming. He said he didn't want to get into a controversial situation. You can imagine how let down I felt.

I was so mad, I wanted to fire every member of that bank board. And I did, too. One of the first people I asked to serve on the new board was Earl Landers, who had been my Agriculture Vocation mentor at Strawberry High School. At that time, he co-owned the Barnett-Landers John Deere Dealership in Batesville. I always told Earl he was too honest to be an equipment dealer. People took advantage of him.

After the dust settled, and I got a new bank board, Mickey agreed to come to Batesville to be President of First National Bank. It took some doing and some healing of the wounds. I agreed to the $37,000 a year salary, but he did such a good job, I raised him $10,000 a year every year while I owned the bank.

The regulatory authorities are always interested when the management of a bank changes hands. Mickey and I got summoned to Memphis right off the bat, and the first question they asked me was "Why did you buy the controlling interest in this bank." I told them I lived within three miles of where I was born, and my dad always told me if anything was for sale and I had the money to buy it, I should." I told the bank examiners I had the money to buy the bank, and their mouths just fell open. They had never known a farmer who had enough money to buy a bank without having to borrow most of it. Once they realized I didn't view the bank as a cash "kitty" for my own use, but as an honest business venture, they were satisfied.

I did have to learn that owning a bank didn't mean I could interfere with the daily operations. Once I understood that, Mickey and I had a wonderful relationship for the 10 years I owned the bank.

When I bought the bank, it had $44 million in assets and when I sold the bank, 10 years later, the assets were $134 million. In 1982, the bank's assets climbed to over $100 million, and this made banking history in Arkansas. For the first time in Arkansas, there was a $100 million bank headquartered in a city of less than 10,000 population.

Banking laws changed, and we established branches at Hardy, Oil Trough, and Pleasant Plains, and a full-service bank at Newark. I took a bull dozer and cleared the land myself for the bank at Newark and a branch at Batesville.

I sold the bank in April 1984. As I look back, I realize it was one of the biggest mistakes I ever made. I had turned the farming operation over to my son, Donald, and to my then son-in-law about the same time. I had too much time and energy on my hands.

In August after I sold the bank, I became co-owner of the Lockhart and Thompson Grain Elevator, and I became co-owner of the Augusta Barge Company. The Barge Company had 19 barges and two tug boats, and shipped crops down the White River to the Mississippi River. From there some of the barges went north to Chicago, and others went downstream to New Orleans and through the inter-coastal waterways to Brownsville, Texas. The port at Brownsville is an open port, so once the barge was unloaded there in a huge warehouse, the shipment could go directly into Mexico.

Once when I was in a warehouse in Mexico City, I looked up and saw stacks of soybeans in bags that had E. R. Coleman Farms, Dowdy, Arkansas, stamped on them. I just had to grin.

I also started investing in post offices. At one time, I owned 25 post offices, plus the Took Gathings Federal Building in Jonesboro, but I didn't have the patience to see the return on the investment.

* * *

Jim Williams and I did have an interesting experience checking out a post office in Eastern Kentucky one time. I owned part of my son Donald's airplane, a Beechcraft Bonanza, and I asked Jim if he would fly me around on some of my business trips. He said he would, but he had to be the one to decide if the airplane and the weather were safe to go.

On our way to Kentucky, we had a layer of clouds we were able to fly above. We couldn't see the ground the entire flight.

The airport didn't have any radio facilities, but the airplane had LORAN, a long-range navigational system using longitude and latitude. That was before GPS came into being. We knew that if we couldn't see the airport through the clouds, we would have to go on to Lexington and make an instrument approach and fly underneath the clouds to the other airport. (Not a good idea because the area was so mountainous. There would be no place to land.)

When Jim thought the airport should be underneath us. He had me look through the broken clouds, and sure enough, it was there. The only problem was that they had dozed off the top of the mountain and put a runway on it. The runway was exactly as long as the top of the mountain.

We landed safely and called a cab. It took 45 minutes to get down the mountain and 45 minutes to get back up. We finished our business and took off just at sundown. Jim told me that once we got started down that runway there would be no stopping. If we were not airborne by that time, we would be in serious trouble, as there was no place to land. Obviously, we had a successful take-off, and it took four hours to fly back to Batesville, Arkansas, in a single-engine airplane at night.

That certainly beat the time Donald and I crashed a small plane into a soybean field near O'Neal. We clipped a power line that belonged to Arkansas Power and Light. The plane was demolished, and no one, including us, could believe we got out alive. Sheriff Noel Baldridge said, "I don't see how they walked away from it. The good Lord was smiling at them." Donald did have a leg injury and I had hit my head real hard, but neither injury was serious.

# A Long Way from Dowdy

One rewarding experience that came to us was back in the early '70s. Florene and I were selected to go on a People-to-People goodwill tour. President Eisenhower started this years ago where business people from this country representing different businesses would go in a group to other parts of the world on a 30-day trip. We'd take our ideas to them, and we would pick up ideas from them. In other words, we would see how they farmed, and they would learn how we farmed.

We went on this trip with Dr. Woody Miley from the University of Arkansas. He is a good agronomist, a good farm man. He knows his soils. He knows production. He knows crops and varieties and fertilizer, and he knows land. He is just one of the best.

We were selected to go on that trip as representatives of agriculture from the State of Arkansas and the United States. There were about 30 of us in the group. We flew from San Francisco to Alaska and then on a 17-hour, non-stop flight to Australia. We landed in Sidney, which is on the eastern edge of Australia. We were scattered out to different farmsteads in that community. We were taken right in by the family on that farm. We slept in their beds, ate at their tables, and visited with them, just as we would want them to do at our house in Arkansas.

That was a rewarding trip for us. We visited nearly every aspect and facet of farming in Australia: cotton, rice, cattle, and everything pertaining to agriculture. They had for all of us what you might call a state dinner and meetings at the capital with the heads of the Departments of Agriculture of each of the countries we visited. We were accompanied by the United States Agricultural attaché. That was a pretty big deal for a little farm boy from Dowdy, Arkansas.

One of the farms we visited belonged to a man from San Francisco. He had gone to Australia years earlier and bought about a million acres of land there and developed it. You could look at that farm, and it was obviously well developed. Most of it was irrigated, and it made my mouth water just to look at it. He bought that land for little of nothing when he first went down there.

Knowing me, of course, I could see what I thought I could do if I could just buy some of this land. It was still cheap then. I was so enticed at the prospect, I went to Canberra and got all of the quadrangle maps of all farmland. It's just a rim of land around the eastern edge and in the southern part of Australia where all the farming is done. The rest of the country is called the "outback," and it's just desert going from western Australia north to Perth.

I asked the man what was the chance of a man coming over there and doing what he had done, but on a smaller scale. They have changed the rules over there so that now you can't own as much as he did. You can't buy so much and so on. He thought about it for a while and said, "Well, it could be done. But you'd have to have a family of 10 kids and put 300 acres of land in each kid's name, and that would give you 3,000 acres. To be frank about it, Coleman, you'd have about as much chance as a snowball in Hell."

After we returned, an Australian by the name of Joe Fox came to visit us twice and stayed several days with us both times. We found out that in order to raise money for his first trip, he had trapped and skinned foxes and sold the pelts. Joe and his family were raised Roman Catholic, and when Sunday came, we took Joe with us to church at the Baptist church at

Cord. He didn't have a Bible, so I gave him one. He had a desire to be a good human being and to do right. He was just a good man. Joe and his family are now in the agricultural servicing business that puts out fertilizer and insecticides, and distributes agricultural products and so on. He and his son run the business.

Basically, one of the main things I learned on that trip is that humanity, basic humanity, is the same everywhere you go. People may have different ways of doing things, but they are human beings, just like I am. They have the same hope and aspirations for their homes and their families and their kids as I did. Might be different, but they still had the same love, the same concern, the same wants for their families as I did for mine.

I think New Zealand is one of the best places I ever visited, and I've been around some. I've been to Europe, Australia, and the Fiji Islands, but New Zealand's countryside was clean everywhere I looked. I didn't see any litter. Everybody's home was well kept, regardless of where it was, whether it was in a town or in the countryside. Their fence rows were clean, the fences painted, and the farms clean.

Other than the United States, I think the best place in the world to get a college degree in agriculture is Lincoln University in Christ Church, New Zealand. Those people know what they are doing. As I remember when I was there, unemployment was two percent. Everybody worked; everything was clean. New Zealand was just one of the prettiest, most progressive places I've ever known.

When we left New Zealand, we had quite an unexpected experience. We were headed to the Fiji Islands, and we called a taxi. The taxi driver asked us what airline we were flying. We told him the name of it was Air Pacific, and he said, "Oh, my! We call that Air Pathetic." Sure enough, that's the way it turned out, and it scared us some. When we got to the airport, we were loaded onto that plane. The weather was humid, and the plane had no air-conditioning. It was a two-engine plane. When the pilot was ready, he cranked up the engine on the right-hand side, and it just purred like a kitten. It cranked up just fine. Then he cranked and cranked and cranked, but the engine on the left-hand side wouldn't start.

Directly, a mechanic and his crew came on board carrying screwdrivers, wrenches, tool boxes, and whatever else they would use to do something or another. Then they would crank and crank and crank again, but they never did get that engine started.

By that time, everybody was wringing wet with sweat, and everybody—including me—was ready to get off that plane. So I guess that was God's blessing to us that that thing didn't start, because it might have quit in midair and crashed and killed us all. They loaded us on another plane. The taxi driver was right: it was Air Pathetic.

I will never forget when we landed on the island of Suva. That was the hottest, most humid place I have ever been. It just seemed as if someone had turned a tea kettle up my britches leg. That's the way it felt. It was just like hot steam from a tea kettle going right up my leg.

The people of Fiji just didn't have anything. It was still just out in the boondocks. But there was some of the finest land you could ever see. As we would drive across that level, black alluvial-looking land, it would just make my mouth water. Boy, I would have loved to put that land into production. As far as the eye could see, it was in swamp grass, or bull grass as I call it, and no one was doing anything with it.

That night at the state dinner, I was seated next to the Secretary of Agriculture who also was the Minister of Finance, Banking, and Land Development or Reclamation. I told him what I had done in America with that type of land and how I had put that land into rice production, pumping water and irrigation and all of that. He really warmed up to me. He sat right there and said, "Mr. Coleman, would you be interested in coming to Suva, to the Fiji Islands?" He said he controlled the money and the banks and all the land in Fiji. He said that if I would come to Suva, come to the Fiji Islands, he'd help me put that land into production. In other words, I could just write my own ticket, that money was no problem. I thought about it for a long time, and I think I could have done it. He even offered to fly me back and forth for 30 days at a time.

When I got back to Arkansas, the man in Fiji wrote me letters trying to persuade me to come back to Fiji and take on that job. That might have been one of the most rewarding things I could have ever done in my life, but I didn't do it.

One of the funny things that happened in the Fiji Islands came when we were crossing the island. There were no roads to speak of, just some dirt trails. We were riding in an old bus-type vehicle that had no windows. It was strictly open air. At the bottom of the hills, there would be these little ravines where they would have a little patch of rice. The local farmers would trap the water coming down the hillsides in the bottom of these little ravines and plant rice there.

As we were coming around a curve one day, there was a little rice field about half an acre in size, and there was a man and his wife in the middle of it. The man had a water buffalo and a forked stick for a plow. He was trying to plow that piece of ground, and they were doing it in the mud, in the water, and he was in mud about knee deep. That dadgum buffalo had lain down out there in the mud. The man was trying to get that bull up out of that mud to pull his plow, and the bull would not do it. His wife was out there up to her knees in mud setting the rice out one stalk at a time.

I said to the bus driver, "Man, I want you to stop. I want to take a picture of that." Then I said, "If I had that hot stick I've got at home, I'd stick that to that bull, and in that wet water, man, he would flat come out of there." Then I added, "And on top of that, if I had a wife who would do what that woman is doing, I'd really have it made." Florene spoke up and said, "Yeah, and if you would do what he's doing, I'll do what she's doing."

Another thing I remember on that trip is that the capital city of Suva is on a small island. From there, we could look up to the north of the town and on top of a hill there was a big fine mansion sitting up there. Strangely enough, the mansion was actually on a different island. Raymond Burr of TV fame owned that island, which consisted of about five acres and a hill with a mansion on top. He had to go a long way to have a summer house.

In August 1990, we were selected as part of the Arkansas People to People Agricultural Mission to Central Europe. During the 15-day trip, we visited the towns and surrounding countryside of Belgrade, Yugoslavia; Budapest, Hungary; Vienna and Salzburg, Austria; Munich, Frankfurt, and Wiesbaden, Germany; and Lucerne, Interlaken, and Berne, Switzerland.

One private trip we took still takes my breath away, even now, when I think about it. Our daughter Kathryn and her husband, Larry May, were living in South Korea. Larry was working on an atomic energy plant there. Florene and I, along with Carol Beth and her two daughters and our daughter-in-law, Deann, went to visit them. Our plane was just 30 minutes ahead, on the same air route, as a KAL plane that was shot down by North Korea for allegedly violating North Korean air space. That was just too close for comfort. We were gone for 30 days, and we also visited Hong Kong where I took the ladies on a shopping spree.

On all of these trips, we knew we were a long way from Dowdy, Arkansas.

# Stories from the Black River

Although life was hard, there was always something going on that broke the monotony of life and gave us a chance to laugh.

One unique thing that's happened here in our community was that there was a cotton gin powered by oxen. Well, you might ask how that could be. The oxen were put up on a big round platform, and as the oxen walked around and around on the platform, the thrust from their legs and their feet turned the wheel. Then the wheel transferred that power to the cotton gin. At one time from Strawberry to Newark to Batesville, there were seven cotton gins.

At one time we had a one-row planter. We had a little patch of ground down on the creek that Daddy had hired Henry Huff to clear. It was about the size of a three-acre block. Daddy had Lem McDaniels laying that off to plant crops. They would lay it off with a plow stock and a mule and then they would come along and run this one-row planter right down in the furrow and plant corn. He had Benny Lance driving one mule and the planter, and Len laying it off with a plow stock. We were down in another field working, and we looked up and saw Benny Lance just stepping it off down the field in a hurry. He said, "Win, I'll tell you what, you need to go up there and look at what Lem is doing. He is making the awfulest mess you ever seen in your life. Them's the crookedest rows I ever saw. I don't want to plant that."

But Daddy said he would not go look. He said, "Well, Benny, I tell you what. Wherever Lem plows, you plant." So that solved that problem. Benny protested, but Daddy's position remained the same. As it turned out, you'd never seen corn rows like that. Some of those corn rows were six inches apart and some were three feet apart, but we still harvested a crop from that field.

* * *

Although the family has given me permission to tell this story, I am using fictitious names to tell it. This happened after I was married. One night, Sally came to my door at 3:00 a.m. Sally was the fourth wife of Bud, and the only one who had settled him down at all. Bud, however, was known to go on a bender once in a while. When I opened the door, Sally said, "Ewell, Bud is out here in the car, and he is drunk, and I want you to go with me down to Curie Creek. Bud says he has drowned a man down there in the creek." The Curie Creek ran down by Turkey Hill at that time. Sally said, "I want you to go with me down there and see if that's true. So I told her I would. I got up and put on my boots and got a shovel so I could punch around to see if I could find the body in the creek. I went out to the car and said, "Bud, what has happened?" Bud said, "Ewell, I've drowned a man. I've killed him. I've drowned him down there in the creek a while ago." Bud began to tell what he looked like. He said the man was the tallest human he'd ever seen and had long greasy hair. Bud said he got into a fight with the man and drowned him. "I held him under the water until he blubbered. He's dead!"

I agreed to go down there, Bud, Sally, and me. When we got there, I got out of the car and crawled down to the creek. The water was only about knee deep. I punched in that old creek all the way up and down the creek for a good way, and I couldn't find anything. So I came back to the old bridge where it crossed the creek, and it looked as if somebody had sat on the bridge, because there was a spot that had mud and water on it. It looked like somebody had come up out of the creek bank and sat on the bridge.

After I couldn't find any body, I figured out what had happened. Bud had a habit of getting drunk at night by himself. He'd just get drunk and park his car and just pass out. I went back to the car and said, "Bud, there ain't nobody down there in the creek! You didn't drown anybody." "Oh, yes, I did! I drowned him. I held him under until he blubbered." I said, "Bud, what has happened is you stopped your car right here on this Turkey Hill Road, and you were drunk, and you got out of your car, and you didn't know where you were, or what you were doing. You went over and sat on the bridge, and you fell off the bridge and like to drown yourself. You can tell where you crawled out up the creek bank." I told him that he thought he was drowning someone else, but he was really about to drown himself.

Bud would have no part of that version, which is what really had happened. Still drunk, Bud went to Cord the next day and told everybody how he had drowned that guy down in the creek last night. Thankfully, nobody believed him.

* * *

People had to make their own entertainment in those days, and shooting matches were one of them. I remember Grissom Phillips who was about five years older than I was. Grissom was a good hunter and a good sportsman, but he beat anything you ever saw when it came to shooting a gun. I remember he could stick a match in a fence post and light it from about 50 feet away with a bullet from a .22 rifle. He could also blow out a match with a bullet from the same distance without hitting the match. It would just whiz right by. You could throw a marble up into the air, and Grissom would fire, and that marble would come down in itty bitty pieces. I couldn't have hit a marble with a shotgun.

* * *

Communities would put together baseball teams. There was one at Cord and another one at Dowdy, which a lot of people called Punkin Center. (It got that name because so many people in the area raised pumpkins to feed to their cattle.) We had a pretty good team. Mr. Luther Melton was the manager. That was back when Monroe Douglas and Pete Douglas and Joe Inman were living here. Monroe was a really good catcher. Pete and Joe were pitchers. They were a good combination. Pete had a slow, wide curve ball. Joe could throw a really fast ball that, when it got right at you, would drop to the ground. I think they called it a fast drop ball. They didn't let anybody steal second base on Monroe. If you left first base to go to second base, he would throw you out every time.

Mr. Luther, who just loved baseball and got a real kick out of it, would put the ball team in the back end of an old iron-wheeled wagon and go around to different communities to play baseball. Most of the games were played on Sunday afternoon.

Up north of Punkin Center was a black community called Driftwood or Little Africa. The community adopted the name Driftwood because black families would just drift into the woods there. If someone who arrived didn't volunteer any information, none was asked. Arthur Montgomery, a descendent of one of the families living there, says that 50 black families lived there in one little colony at one time. There was a lot of love in the community for each other. Arthur's father, Savoy, along with his three brothers, farmed 138 acres there at Driftwood. Other families in the area owned small pieces of land, and they also hired out to the Sloan and the Penn families, both of whom had large farms in Lawrence County. In a lot of cases, they were not paid wages but would swap work.

The community was a close-knit group, and it was share-and-share-alike in their community. One time, the families went together and jointly purchased a car, a Model T. The car belonged to the entire community, not just one person. A beloved member of that community, Aunt Tess, who had been a slave, was the midwife for the entire area for both black and white families. Driftwood had its own school house, which doubled as church on Sunday. It was the Bethel A.M.E. Church and sat right in the middle of the Driftwood Community. It was common in a rural area for a building to serve as both a school and a church. The white folks used the building for a Sunday church service in the mornings, and the black folks used it for a church service on Sunday afternoons.

Driftwood also had a baseball team and a good one. They would come to Punkin Center and play the Punkin Center baseball team. (Attitudes about race had softened a lot since 1930 and earlier.) I remember very well a young man named Yancey Montgomery was on that team, and if he ever got on first base, it would be an automatic score. Man, he could run like lightning. He could steal a base on you with you standing there watching him. No one could tag him out. He would dodge them or run under them or slide under them or do whatever it took. When he got on first base, you knew what was going to happen.

Harm Montgomery, Yancey's uncle, used to work for us a lot at the sawmill, and he worked loading crossties in boxcars primarily in the tie yard. Harm and some of the other men had a routine of how to load the boxcars. Two men would lift a 7 x 9 crosstie, and Harm would walk under it and lay it on his shoulder and walk up a gangplank with it on his shoulder and then throw it over into the boxcar. Harm did that day after day. He was a man of tremendous strength. When he died over at Hoxie, my mother and daddy went to his funeral, and they were the only two white people there. Dad really cared a lot about Harm Montgomery.

Savoy Montgomery was one of the community leaders at Little Africa-Driftwood, and well-respected in Batesville. At one time, Savoy managed the Marvin Hotel in downtown Batesville for a Mr. Polk. Mr. Charles Barnett, from Batesville, hired Savoy to drive him around the state on various business trips. One time they were coming back from a meeting and arrived at Harrison, Arkansas, at suppertime. When Mr. Barnett found out that the restaurant refused to serve Savoy a meal, even out the back door, Mr. Barnett got up and walked out of the restaurant. Mr. Barnett told the owner of the restaurant that if he couldn't serve Savory, he couldn't serve him, either. Savoy said he would never set foot in Harrison again, and didn't. Savoy is the father of Arthur Montgomery who just retired, after 37 years, as the head of the Independence County Employment Security Office. His son, Andy, is a loan officer at one of the Batesville banks.

The ancestors of the Montgomery family were slaves, with the last name of Flemmons, from North Carolina. The Flemmons family was sold to a Dr. Watkins, who brought them to Independence County.

One event that everyone, black and white, looked forward to was the 4th of July picnic at Driftwood. People came from miles around. The community would barbecue a pig and sell plates of barbecue and glasses of lemonade as a fund raiser, although there wasn't much money to be made. As Savoy always said, "Everybody had the same amount of poor." In the afternoon, there would be a baseball game of whites against blacks. The ball was made of string that the boys in Driftwood had pulled from their yarn socks. The community built an outdoor dance floor, about 30- to 40-foot square, and got Frank Cravens, one of the best fiddlers in the area, to play the fiddle for everyone to dance in the evening. After the fiddlers had about three shots of moonshine in them, the fiddles would really sing. The picnic was the highlight of the summer.

\* \* \*

One Halloween there at Cord, when my dad was a kid, some of the boys "borrowed" a wagon and took the wagon apart, piece by piece. It's been told Elmer West helped do this. Then they carried it up to the top of Mr. Harrington's Store, and put the wagon back together right up astraddle the roof. The next morning, there set the wagon right up on the top of the store building. Of course to get it down, it had to be taken apart piece by piece, and that was pretty mischievous to put the wagon up on the roof. But it was good clean fun, and everyone got a laugh over it.

There was a man who I'll call Mr. Smith for this story. Everybody thought of him as an educated man. He was pretty smart when it came to some things, but not others. Back then, there used to be a cattle pen down at Newark, and people would ship cattle, hogs, sheep, or whatever to St. Louis. Mr. Smith shipped a bunch of sheep to market one week. Later, Mr. Smith got a letter saying they had received his sheep, and they had been sold, but the sheep didn't bring enough to pay the freight and the commission. A bill was attached. Mr. Smith wrote them back and said, "Well, thank you for your letter. I don't have any money, but I've got some more sheep I can send you." He really believed that was the solution, not understanding it would just put him further in the hole.

The Democratic Primary always was a source of interest and talk. My grandfather Campbell Greer was a community-minded man. One time, some of the "powers-that-be" in Batesville, which was the county seat, came out to Cord and told his brother, Walter Greer, that he was to take the approved list of candidates around to the various small communities in the area, like Lockhart and Turkey Hill. Uncle Walter was a well-known guy and was active in a lot of things. At that time, politics wasn't much different than they are today. Uncle Walter was to tell those people how to vote. Now there weren't any roads from Cord to Lockhart or Turkey Hill. There were just wagon trails through the woods in the bottoms.

Uncle Walter was to urge the people in those tiny communities to get in their wagons and go to Cord and vote for a certain man for sheriff. I won't give the man's name, but he was in charge of and ran most of the businesses in the eastern end of the county. Uncle Walter said, "Why, I can't do that. I wouldn't vote for that guy, no way." He also said he knew the folks up at Turkey Hill "hate that man's guts" and wouldn't vote for him. Uncle Walter said if he took that list up there and told them to vote for the man, "They will kill me! Man, I just can't do that."

The man from Batesville kept on talking to Uncle Walter and somehow persuaded him to do that. The next morning, he took the list up to those people, and when they saw the list, and who was running for sheriff, they said, "Walter, have you lost your mind? We know you don't like him any better than we do, and we're not going to vote for him. You are out of your mind to come up here and ask us to do that." Walter said, "I'll tell you what let's do. Just go vote for the SOB, and maybe he will get elected, and somebody will shoot him." ("SOB" doesn't mean "Sweet Old Boy.") That's how Uncle Walter got off the hook. Lucky for the man, he didn't win.

Florene and I always dug potatoes on the Fourth of July. And when we would get through, we would go to Currie Creek with Van Doyne and Winona, my brother and sister, to cool off. There was a pool of water there that was so deep, you could hardly find the bottom. Florene like to have drowned there one Fourth of July. She got out too far, and I was trying to get to her. She's always told me I just let her go, which wasn't the truth.

She has always kidded me about hoping she would drown. She was accusing me of not trying to get to her, but I was trying my best. Luckily, Van Doyne, who was a better swimmer, jumped in and got to her. She would have drowned if it hadn't been for him, I guess, and I was grateful to him. I was doing all I could, however, but I'm not a very good swimmer.

# More Tales from the River

I've heard my dad tell this story many times, although it happened before my time. A Mr. W. N. Osborne owned Osborne's General Store in Cord. It's where the post office is now, but at one time it served as a type of Wal-Mart where you could buy anything, including coffins. If you needed a loan for a crop, Mr. Osborne would give you one. He had a sign that said: "We will take care of you from the cradle to the grave."

Mr. Osborne used to tell that in the early days of his store, the men did the grocery shopping, and the wives stayed in the wagon while the husbands shopped. Well, someone had to watch the mules.

Back then, you could go to the general store in the wintertime and hear all the stories, news, and gossip of the community, as everyone sat around an old wood-burning stove. There was a crowd there everyday in the wintertime. Dad said this was around 1915, and it was so cold everything was frozen tight as a jug. A Mr. Beck came into the store and said he had driven his team and old iron-wheel wagon, loaded with his family and their belongs, across the river on the ice. The stove-side group just didn't believe him. There was ice in the river, and the ferry couldn't run, but they made light of his story, and Mr. Beck got really mad. But it really had frozen solid. Risking his family's life driving the wagon across the ice, that could give away any minute, meant he either had a lot of faith or was stupid.

Although it is rare for the Black River to freeze completely, it often overflowed. Sometimes, people had to plant their crops several times because of the overflow. The flood of 1927 was the one that my father talked about a lot.

Back then, there weren't any roads through the river bottoms. There was just an old muddy trail through the bottoms from Cord in the hills over to Jackson County. There was an old wooden ferry across the river at Elgin, which was important because there was a big cotton gin there on the river at Elgin, plus a store and seven or eight houses. The boats would come up the river as far as Elgin and unload the supplies. That's how folks got their goods. There weren't any real roads, just dirt trails. A wagon and a team could get through the bottoms up to the foothills, but a car couldn't have made it.

During the flood of 1927, the river overflowed so much that they loaded families, with their mules and wagons, onto the ferry, and men used poles to push the ferry up the old oxen trail all the way across the bottoms. They unloaded the families at the foothills near Cord. During that flood, the Black River ran through Jackson County, and my dad paddled a boat down a lane that ran by James' Store. Nowadays, when you tell folks about his paddling a boat right through Jackson County, they won't believe you.

The Black River was bad to overflow. I've been told of ones in 1913 and 1927. I remember the big floods of 1937 and 1945, and a lot of smaller floods in between. Over the years, the land has been cleared and the overflows aren't as bad. However in the 1982 flood, some call it the flood of the century, the water from the Black River came to the bottom of the hill where my house is located. I had a 40-acre catfish farm down just below the hill. The river water overflowed the catfish farm, and all the catfish swam off. I always said I was just one overflow away from the poor house.

With all those overflows, floods, and generally swampy land, there were thousands of mosquitoes, and malaria was rampant. I can't begin to tell you how much quinine I have drunk in my lifetime. It would number in the gallons.

Without actual roads or bridges, people had to have a way to get their cotton, their basic cash crop, to market. The ferries up and down the Black River played an essential part in moving the cotton to Elgin, Swifton, Tuckerman, or anyplace else that had a gin. Records show that in the 1890s, a Mr. Smith ran a ferry on the Black River at the mouth of the Strawberry River.

There have been numerous ferries on the Strawberry and Black Rivers. Starting at Black Rock, there were ferries at Powhatton, Gibson, and Whitow. The Partee Ferry was north of the mouth of the Strawberry, and then on down the Black River there were ferries at Lockhart, Elgin, and Jacksonport.

A ferry was propelled by the river current but controlled by a cable stretched from a windlass on a side bank of the river and anchored to, usually, a large tree on the opposite bank. The windlass allowed for the cable to be adjusted. A large wooden drum acted as a spool upon which the rope or cable could be coiled. A lever on the drum allowed a man to turn it and tighten or loosen the cable as need be. The lever was secured with a stob at the desired tension. Ferry boats were usually 12 to 14 feet wide and about 25 feet long. They were large enough to hold two wagons and teams at one time.

Each ferry had two sets of pulleys and trace chains. The pulleys slid upon the cable, and the chains kept the boat square to the cable. The current, of course, propelled the boat. Going across the river, the chain at the back was loosened, and on the return the trip, the chain lengths were reversed. The ferries were licensed by the County Courts, which also set the rates for passage. In 1918, the records show that the licensing fee for the ferries at Lockhart, Elgin, and the Strawberry River where it emptied into the Black River was $5.00 a year. By 1939, the fee had reached $100.00 a year. The court also set certain standards for the operators of the ferries. From the boat landing to the top of high ground on each said approach was to have an elevation not to exceed one foot perpendicular to 10 feet. Plus, the approaches had to be planked with good lumber. In 1918, it cost a man 10 cents to go across on foot, or 20 cents round trip. If the man had a horse, it was 20 cents one way and 35 cents round trip. A four-house team and a wagon cost 75 cents one way, and a $1.25 round trip.

The first wooden ferry at Elgin was owned by Mr. J. O. Taylor. A generation later, A. C. Tims, who had married into the Taylor family, ran the ferry. By that time, it was made of steel. The first day A. C. ran the ferry, he had to move his cable and tied it to a large mulberry stump on top the hill. I crossed the river that day with a big load of soybeans. Just as the front wheels of my truck reached the dirt bank on the other side, I heard a noise and looked back and the mulberry stump had turned loose and shot 40 feet into the air. The boat slid right out from under me and dumped me, my truck, and trailer into the river. The water came up to within three inches of the soybeans. It took a tow truck to haul all of that out of the river. When the county finally got real roads and the ferry closed, it had been in the Taylor family for over a hundred years.

In the early days of the county, people said that steamboats could go up the Black River all the way to Popular Bluff, Missouri. It's a fact the steamboats could go as high as Pocahontas. One of the steamboats was built at Pocahontas and was named *The Pocahontas*. The river is now so filled in with silt that it is impossible for steamboats to do that.

People would raft logs down the river since there were no roads to speak of, or equipment to move them otherwise.

What were called fast boats would come up the Black River and leave loaded down with barrels and jugs of moonshine whiskey. The shipment was then taken down the waterways and up the Mississippi to St. Louis. It was big business!

\* \* \*

Probably the most exciting thing that ever happened in eastern Independence County, and to my family, was when the bank at Black Rock got robbed. Mr. Jay Meyers, the owner of the bank, was there the day it happened. (He also owned the bank at Walnut Ridge.) As soon as the robbers left, Mr. Meyers did not go to the sheriff, but went instead to get Mr. Sam Payne, who lived close by and always carried a gun. Everyone said Sam wasn't afraid of the devil.

Mr. Payne got into Mr. Meyers' car and took the butt of his gun and broke out the windshield in order to get a clear shot. The robbers got to the edge of the Black River before Meyers and Payne caught up with them. A boy, whose last name was Herring, was fishing at the edge of the river near the mouth of the Strawberry River, and he happened to have a john boat. The robbers asked if he could paddle them across to the opposite shore. He said that of course he could, and did. When they got to the other side, the robbers asked him how much they owed him. He told them that they didn't owe him anything. They had the boy take off his cap and filled it full of coins. The boy said, "You guys must have robbed a bank"— not knowing that they had.

The robbers made their way on down the west side of the river and to Crews Bend, of "moonshining" fame. Twelve-year-old Pearl Crews was in the front yard, and when she saw the armed men coming, she ran into the house yelling, "Aunt May, Aunt May, the 'revenoors' are outside, and somebody is goin' to be killed." Being an IRS agent in the backwoods, moonshining areas of rural Arkansas was a dangerous and sometimes deadly occupation.

The robbers bypassed the Crews' house and, about dusk, arrived at my father's house. Since there was no way of knowing about the bank robbery, my dad answered the knock at the door. A man said he had had car trouble and asked Dad to take him, in the truck, to Batesville. It was wintertime, and Dad had already drained the water from the radiator as there was no such thing as anti-freeze in those days. Dad tried to reason with the man and told him he couldn't do it because his truck would freeze. The man threatened him, so Dad filled the radiator with water, and Mother brought a quilt out to put over the car's hood trying to keep the water from freezing. Then one by one the other men started coming out of the woods up to the truck. The lead man demanded that Mother get quilts for the other men to wrap around themselves in the back of the truck.

Dad was low on gas, so they stopped at Mr. Weaver's store at Charlotte, and one of the robbers went in with him. Dad said, "Mr. Weaver I am in a lot of trouble. This man here, with a gun pointed at me, is making me take him and the others to Batesville. I reckon I don't have a choice because they are the meanest bunch of sons-of-bitches I have ever seen." Dad was scared, but said that with the robber standing right there with a gun stuck in his ribs.

Dad got the gas, and Mr. Weaver had a phone and called Charley Osborne at his store. The odd thing was that the County Sheriff, Jake Engles, was standing right there in Osborne's store when the call came in. Mr. Weaver told Charlie that he was sure that Win had the Black Rock robbers in his truck headed to Batesville. No one did anything. The Sheriff had a good car, and probably could have run over Daddy three or four times between Cord and Batesville. My opinion and my dad's was that he didn't want to catch them. Maybe he was like Pearl Crews and thought somebody was probably going to get killed, and he didn't want it to be him. It was probably a good thing, because if road blocks had been set up, Dad might have been shot.

When they got to Batesville, the robbers wanted dad to take them to a certain place in west Batesville, but Dad told him that if he drove down the middle of Main Street, the police would stop them for sure. His truck didn't have any taillights. So they had him drop them off at the water tower, which was on a hillside at the edge of town. There is a house right by the water tower, and the robbers went into the man's house and made him take them to his car and drive them way out of town. They then kicked him out of his car and put him afoot.

The car was found three days later in Oklahoma City. The police took Dad to look at police lineups in St. Louis, Dallas, and Oklahoma City, but he never saw anyone in the lineups he had seen that night. The bank robbery at Black Rock was never solved.

# Memories of Independence County, Arkansas

## Old Time Remedies

Don Coleman told me about my great Granddad Coleman when he came back home from the civil war. All the men said they had itch and lice all over them, and were in pretty much rundown condition. So my great Granddad Coleman went to where the women had made lye soap. Lye soap was made from lard from when they killed hogs. The lard was mixed with lye from the ash hoppers. An ash hopper was a V-shaped container where ashes were put. They would pour water over the ashes in the hopper, and the lye would run out of the bottom of the trough. They would then take that and boil it with the meat drippings to make lye soap. After it was cooked and cooled, they could cut it out of the pot with a knife. At the very bottom was a type of jelly that might have been pure lye. Granddad Coleman took some of that jelly, thinking it was the same as soap, and rubbed himself down with it. It set him afire and liked to have burned him up. The first thing they knew was that they didn't know where Granddad was. He had run off to Montgomery Springs just North of Cord. That's where they found him sitting in the spring up to his neck. He was probably free of the lice for sure, but he never tried that again.

\* \* \*

My dad told about the time when he was 16 or so, and he had the itch. He had heard that pokeberry roots were good for the itch, so he went out and dug up a bunch of pokeberry roots and boiled them down in a great big pot. He lowered himself into the pot of pokeberry juice, and it was just like Great Granddad Coleman. It set him on fire and liked to burn him up. I don't know whether or not it killed the itch (it was pretty strong stuff), but he never tried that again, either.

# Presbyterian Influence in Independence and Lawrence Counties

Lawrence County, Arkansas, was sparsely settled in the mid 1800s. Houses averaged two to five miles apart. In the winter of 1848, a man by the name of J. Fleming, who lived on Cypress Creek near the edge of the Black River bottoms, went to help his neighbor by the name of Parsley kill hogs. Mr. Fleming lived about five miles away from the Parsley farm. The men worked all day butchering hogs. It got late, so the Parsley family invited Mr. Fleming to stay for supper, which he did.

When Mr. Fleming did not return home that night, the family was not alarmed. They assumed it had gotten late, and he had stayed the night. By mid-day they realized something was wrong and went in search of him. They followed an old stock trail to the Parsley farm. They first found one of Fleming's shoes, then bits of his clothes, and later they found three dead wolves, one had the butcher knife in it, broken off at the hilt. Apparently Mr. Fleming had lost his fight with the fourth wolf. All they found of Mr. Fleming was his skeleton. His grave began the Old Lebanon Cemetery. People at his funeral donated enough money to buy the surrounding two acres. That area was filled up by 1889, so two more acres were acquired.

In 1852, the Old Lebanon Church, of the Cumberland Presbyterian faith, was built adjacent to the cemetery. Mr. Isaiah Warren was the force in establishing the church. This man started the church and school at the Old Stone School House at Dowdy. He had brought his family to this area by covered wagon from Winston-Salem, North Carolina. They settled on Webb Branch just before it empties into Curie Creek about three-quarters of a mile from where the Stone School House now stands. Mr. Warren was known for saying he was not going to live in a community that didn't have a church or a school.

In December 1852, Burgess Thomason deeded four acres of his land in the Northwest corner of Section 17, Range 2W, Township 16 to the Lebanon Church. The Lebanon Church was the first Cumberland Presbyterian Church built in Lawrence County. It was built of hewn logs with an elevated front. There was an upper balcony where the slaves could sit during the worship service. John Casper, Burgess Thomason, John Mitchell, and Anthony Cozort took responsibility for building this church. Mr. Cozort made the nails for the building from worn out horse shoes. Most of the founding members of the church had moved to that area from Rowan County, North Carolina, in 1851.

When the church was completed, the date was set for dedication. The day of the dedication turned out to be cold and rainy. The preacher came on horseback from Old Jackson. When he got there, the congregation consisted of three people. The preacher announced he would not preach to so small a congregation. John Casper stood up and asked him, "If you had a bunch of hogs in the woods, and you went to feed them, and after calling, only two or three hogs came, would you feed them, or would you take the corn back home because the whole bunch did not come?" Mrs. Casper then quoted the scripture, "Feed my lambs." At this point the preacher got up and preached, which was considered one of the best sermons ever preached in that church. He used the text: "If you love me, feed my lambs" as his theme, and the sermon lasted two and a half hours.

Original members of the church were Burgess Thomason, Elizabeth H. Blackwell (wife of Benjamin Blackwell), Sara M Blackwell (who later married John Casper), and Mary Ann and Anthony Cozort. Benjamin Blackwell and Anthony Cozort were the deacons of the church.

The Church House was also used as a school building. Mrs. Reanor (Rena) Cozort taught the first school. She would walk two miles each day, carrying her shoes and stockings until nearly in sight of the school. Then she would put them on. That was her way of making her shoes last longer. Only two text books were used: the Bible and the Blue Back Speller Book.

Revis Casper, the grandson of the above mentioned John Casper, was my favorite teacher of all the teachers I ever had.

Oscar Warren, son of Isaiah Warren, was a founding father of the Hopewell Cumberland Presbyterian Church at Cord. Church records indicate a mission of the Hopewell Church was established at the Stone School House. Mr. Warren built the church/school house himself, and he served as both the preacher and the school teacher. He also developed a large and successful farming operation. His farm ran from the top of Curie Creek near Cave City to where the creek empties into the Black River on the eastern edge of the county. The Warren, Pickens, and Forrester families were all strong Presbyterian families in that area.

Mr. Oscar Warren had three children—Eugene, Blake, and Allie Warren. Allie told me that her father had both a degree in law and in medicine. She went on to become a registered nurse and spent her entire life as a psychiatric nurse at the Arkansas Mental Hospital in Benton, Arkansas.

At different times, Eugene and Blake each served as executive director of the National Cumberland Presbyterian

Church Association. These brothers made church history, as they were the only two brothers to ever hold the highest office in the National Church.

Eugene was elected the Director of the Office of Finance Administration for the National Church Organization. He handled and invested all of the money from church funds, and also managed all their endowments. It has been said that under Eugene's leadership, the church received the best yields ever from their investments. Eugene Warren also sold, from the Cumberland Presbyterian Endowment Fund, a farm in Tennessee to Senator Al Gore, the father of Vice President Al Gore.

The Warren brothers and the Forresters, and others from around Cord, were students at Bethel Presbyterian College in McKensie, Tennessee. They had first been students at the Stone School House at Cord.

J. C. Forrester and his brother Robert were Presbyterian ministers and held high offices in the Church State Association. I want to give honor and thanks to these families who produced four Cumberland Presbyterian ministers, and who rose to the highest ranks in their faith. There has not been enough honor or thanks and recognition for the accomplishments of these men and their families in this area. I consider this "up in pretty high cotton" coming from Web Branch-Dowdy-Cord, in Independence County, Arkansas.

## Batesville, Arkansas
## My Town, My County Seat

Batesville, Arkansas, has a long and fascinating history. The Osage Indians ceded the area to the U.S. Government in 1808. Originally, it was part of Missouri Territory, and the settlement was originally called Poke Creek, which was the second oldest settlement after Arkansas Post. Eleven years later, the area became a part of Arkansas Territory, and one of the earliest settlers was Judge James Woodson Bates, who migrated from Virginia in 1819.

Independence County was created on October 20, 1820, from Lawrence County which had been created by the Missouri Legislature in 1815. Originally, Independence County included what is now Jackson, Izard, Sharp, and Stone Counties. It was named in honor of the Declaration of Independence. The first post office was opened in 1822 with Nathan Cook as post master. In 1824, Poke Creek was renamed Batesville after Judge Bates.

During its early existence, the settlement's economy depended on hides and furs from numerous wild animals that the settlers traded for groceries and other supplies. The beautiful White River played a major role for the settlers, providing navigation, food, and drinking water. Batesville still relies on the White River and credits it as its most valuable natural resource.

Education has long been a part of Batesville's culture. The Batesville Academy was the first academy in the state to be incorporated by a bill signed by Governor Conway on September 26, 1836. Today Lyon College (originally Arkansas College) is a result of that early interest in education by the people in the area, and the college carries on that tradition.

A Mr. Aaron Lyon was one of the first members of Batesville Academy. He came to Batesville in 1822 and taught school there until he entered the mercantile business in 1842.

The White River also played a role in the Civil War. Batesville was an important port, along with the nearby Black River. The town of Batesville had both pro-Union and pro-Southern sympathizers. On May 3, 1862, the town was sized by Union troops under the command of Samuel. R. Curtis.

The Union victory at Elk Horn Tavern in March of that year had opened the door to Northeast Arkansas. A small group of Confederate irregulars led by William O. Coleman (one of my kinfolks) met Brigadier General E. A. Carr's Cavalry. The skirmish occurred near the home of Elisha Baxter, a staunch Unionist and later Governor of Arkansas. Coleman's troops retreated across the river. Many skirmishes occurred in the area, but no major battles ensued. As the Federal troops pushed southward, they were largely unopposed, and they foraged, burned, and pillaged farms and farmland.

Today, Batesville is a thriving community of more than 10,000 people who are engaged in farming, beef cattle production, and poultry. One outstanding attraction is the Independence Regional Museum, which sits at the edge of historic Batesville. It is housed in the former National Guard armory and serves a 12-county area that was at one time part of Independence County.

The museum houses a vast cross section of artifacts, videos, research materials, and a miniature replica of Dowdy, Arkansas, which was constructed by my sister, Winona Coleman Penn. Also in the museum are the original mailboxes and service counter that was in our store at Dowdy.

Many of Batesville's citizens have made significant contributions—not only locally, but also to the state of Arkansas. One name that is known nationally, however, is that of Mark Martin of NASCAR driving fame. Mark got his start right here in Batesville at age 15 when he won his first checkered flag at a feature race here in town. That same year, he became Arkansas' stock car champion. He then started the climb that eventually won him 33 Winston Cups. Mark has a permanent residence here in Batesville and co-owns, with Lance Lander, the Ford Dealership here. Housed within the Ford dealership building is a national NASCAR museum.

There are many reasons why I am proud of Batesville, the county seat of Independence County, and these are just a few of them.

# Bits and Pieces from the Adjoining Lawrence County

A young man by the name of Brooks Penn from Lynn, Arkansas, in Lawrence County was elected to the offices of Lawrence County Judge for 12 years and Treasurer of Lawrence County for eight years. When Mr. Penn campaigned for these offices, he told the people of Lawrence County he was not a politician or a political speaker. His campaign speeches consisted of very few words and went something like this: "I am Brooks Penn from Lynn, Arkansas. All you people know me. If you can vote for me, I will appreciate it. I will try my best to do you a good job." Then Mr. Penn would sit down.

Indeed, Brooks Penn did do a good job. He was one of the best county judges Lawrence County ever had, despite his campaign speeches of very few words.

The most intense political race in Lawrence County history was the race for Lawrence County Judge between Brooks Penn and W. R. Glenn. Both these gentlemen were intelligent, attractive, hard working, honest men from the same small, rural town of Lynn.

Don Hardaway from Strawberry, Arkansas, in Lawrence County is another man who comes to mind. During Mr. Hardaway's lifetime, he was elected to every Lawrence County office, except the offices of county judge and sheriff. Don served Lawrence County 37 years of his life as an elected county official.

# Looking Back. Looking Forward.

Here it is 2007. I'm 82 years old, and I have recently started a new agricultural consulting business, *Leading the Field LLC*, using the latest software and technology to help farmers become profit centers. Some people have called me a "human dynamo," and I guess I just have too much energy to just sit still and be retired.

People have asked me when was the happiest time in my life. It was when the kids were still at home. We were a family, and all of us worked to make the family succeed. That was the happiest time of my life.

# Editor's Note

It was a real privilege to work with E. R. Coleman as he shared the story of his life and accomplishments with me. He is, indeed, a "human dynamo" with incredible energy, intellect, and vision. This book covers only some of the things he has done to improve life in eastern Independence County, in particular, and the entire county as a whole. While working with him, it became obvious he has a great love for Independence County and its people. He has truly been a man with honor.

Mary Frances Hodges

CPSIA information can be obtained
at www.ICGtesting.com
Printed in the USA
FFOW03n1524020315
11425FF